"Margaret Paul's work is [illegible] has been a leader in the field [illegible] for decades and I've seen from my own [illegible] experience the remarkable power of her Inner Bonding work. I've used it in my own life, and I've shared it with many of my clients and students. Inner Bonding is a cutting-edge process for self-love. It gets profound results, and it gets them quickly. Margaret is truly a master, and the Inner Bonding process creates miracles."

—Marci Shimoff, #1 *NY Times* bestselling author,
Happy for No Reason and *Chicken Soup for the Woman's Soul*, and creator of *Your Year of Miracles*

"Dr. Margaret Paul and her work is a magnificent combination of tough love, no nonsense, and brilliance, combined with deep sensitivity, spirituality, and courage, and so is her work. Her *Inner Bonding* program takes us beyond introspection, insights, and interpretations about our past and moves us into the present. There, it provides us with tools to uncover our authentic self and develop our loving and mature adult. Loving of self and others.

"This program will help you liberate yourself and find greater freedom, maturation, peace, joy, and potency of action in the world. It will help you become more of who you were born to be."

—Anat Baniel, Founder of Anat Baniel
Method®NeuroMovement®,
Author of *Move Into Life* and *Kids Beyond Limits*

"Dr. Margaret Paul is a true master of Love. By reconnecting the aspects of the personality that have been marginalized for protective reasons early-on in life, with the essential, Soulful Self for bonding, healing and generating a true loving presence on the planet, she transforms life—right before one's eyes—into deeply meaningful moments of celebrating our wholeness. Her work is timely, profound and completely accessible for everyone. Thank you, Margaret, for sharing your gifts with the world."

—Dr. Sue Morter, Founder Morter Institute
for Bio-Energetics, Author of *The Energy Codes:
The 7 Step System for Awakening Your Spirit,
Healing Your Body and Living Your Best Life*,
Developer of The Energy Codes Personal Development
Coursework, Host GAIA TV Healing Matrix,
Co-Host Your Year of Miracles

6 STEPS TO TOTAL SELF-HEALING

THE INNER BONDING® PROCESS

Margaret Paul, Ph.D.

MEDIA

Published 2021 by Gildan Media LLC
aka G&D Media
www.GandDmedia.com

Front cover design by David Rheinhardt of Pyrographx

Interior design by Meghan Day Healey of Story Horse, LLC

Library of Congress Cataloging-in-Publication Data is available upon request

ISBN: 978-1-7225-0505-9

10 9 8 7 6 5 4 3 2 1

This book is dedicated to Dr. Erika Chopich,
the co-creator of Inner Bonding,
and to my higher guidance,
who brought us Inner Bonding,
and who is always here guiding me
moment-by-moment.

Acknowledgments

I am deeply indebted to my Divine guidance, who is always here for me and who writes, creates, and teaches through me. I would not know how to live my life without the love, compassion, comfort, and wisdom of my Divine guidance.

I feel very grateful for Dr. Erika Chopich, the co-creator of Inner Bonding, for her brilliance, creativity, and wisdom in always knowing the answers when I come to her for help. She is an amazingly powerful and loving person, and I feel deeply blessed that she is in my life.

I am grateful for my agent, Dan Strutzel, of Inspired Productions, for his belief in Inner Bonding and his support for my work.

I'm grateful for my clients and for participants in my workshops, intensives, and courses. You continue to inspire me and teach me so much by your willingness to learn and grow.

I'm very grateful for the support I receive for my work from many of the people in the organization I belong to, The Transformational Leadership Council, and particularly for Marci Shimoff and Debra Poneman for mentoring me in bringing Inner Bonding further out into the world. Thank you both for your generosity in sharing your experience with me.

I feel blessed by the Inner Bonding Facilitators who have stepped up to the plate to create and teach The Inner Bonding Facilitator Training Program to people from all over the world. You are all doing an amazing job!

Finally, I'm deeply grateful for Inner Bonding. My ongoing practice of Inner Bonding has brought me so much love, peace, joy, fulfillment, and abundant health.

Contents

Preface

This book contains a concise description of the Inner Bonding process, which I have been teaching since 1983. The content is developed from my seminars and workshops with a live audience. It includes exchanges between participants and me, which I have included because they illustrate key issues and difficulties that people may encounter when learning and practicing Inner Bonding.

1

Learning How to Love Myself

I was born on a farm in upstate New York to very clueless parents. In fact, my mother went to a doctor to get birth control three months after they were married and found out she was pregnant. One of the things I always heard is, "You were the best mistake that ever happened." Of course, as a kid, all you hear is "mistake."

I lived on the farm. I have a very good memory, so I can remember being outside in the playpen and feeling an incredible sense of oneness with nature and feeling much peace in being out there. My paternal grandfather was a person whom my mother didn't like at all, and from what I have been told, I was the only person he ever loved. He would come by every day. I remember sitting on his lap, feeling his heartbeat, and feeling the connection; it was very special.

When I was thirteen months old, we left the farm and came to Los Angeles. My parents were very poor. I never saw my grandfather again because he died when I was four. He might have been as heartbroken as I was. Of course, when you are thirteen months old, you don't know that you are the one that has left, so in my mind he left me.

When I was ten, we visited the farm and I said, "My grandfather used to walk down that road." My parents were stunned that I knew that.

After we moved, I got life-threateningly ill; I almost died. When you are young, you develop beliefs, and I developed the belief that if somebody I love leaves, I'm going to die. That laid the groundwork for me to become a very good girl.

We decide fairly young what our protection strategies are going to be. Mine was to be a caretaker, to tune into everybody else, and to make sure everybody else was OK. I learned to ignore my own feelings.

In my household, my mother was quite narcissistic. She was a screamer, and I was the only child, so she screamed at me.

My father was a pretty good father for the first twelve years of my life, and then he got it into his head that it was his right to have sex with me and he became sexually abusive, so I had to stay away from him. Until then, he was the only person I could go to. After age twelve, I was on my own.

My grandmother lived with us, and she was horrible. I always tried to stay away from her as much as I could.

It was a lonely and scary childhood in many ways, because I was very sensitive. The yelling and the indifference to my feelings created a very tense child. By the time I was five, I bit my nails, had a nervous cough, and couldn't sleep. My mother took me to a psychiatrist (because obviously it was *my* problem). I'll never forget the tall, skinny guy who, after talking to me and talking to my mother, said to me, "Tell your mother not to yell at you." I remember thinking, "I am five years old. She is not going to listen to me, so *you* tell her." My next thought was, "I can do a better job than you."

That was the day I decided to do this work, and I've never wavered from it.

Kids and even adults often came to me with their problems. I was the kind of kid who would listen and would be there. I grew up being there for everybody else and not being there for *me*. I became a caretaker.

Caretakers usually come from the wounded, ego part of the self as a form of control, to try to get love and avoid pain. Usually we attract somebody on the other end of the spectrum, who is a taker. The taker says, "It's your responsibility to make me feel I'm OK, validate me, have sex with me, or love me in the way I want to be loved."

The caretaker says, "OK, I'll be that person. I'll take care of you, and I'm going to take my feelings and my inner child and put them in a closet in the hope that you're going to take care of *my* feelings." (Your inner child is your feeling self, your soul essence.)

Caretakers soon learn that that never happens, and after a while they become depleted. They feel like martyrs. That's how I felt: "I'm giving, and everybody else is taking." That's what I grew up with; that's what I knew.

People sometimes ask whether you can be a taker in one area and a caretaker in another. The answer is yes. In a relationship, one person may be the emotional caretaker, while the other is the emotional taker. At the same time, the latter might be the financial caretaker, while the first person is the financial taker. Or one could be the taker and the other the caretaker sexually. In one relation-ship, you might be primarily a taker and primarily a caretaker in another. These are both aspects of the ego wounded self.

When I was being a caretaker, I thought I was being loving. I would congratulate myself and say, "Look how loving I am. Look at what I am doing for everybody." I was Mother Earth for my husband, my parents, my kids—everybody. I thought I was being loving, and it was a shock to realize that I was controlling. Caretaking has an agenda, and any time we are giving with an agenda to get something back, that's controlling.

We can go back and forth. When you are a caretaker, you think you are better. Caretakers think they are better than the takers.

Both roles are forms of control; one is simply a more overt form, whereas the other is more covert. The takers may be getting angry and demanding, and that's overt, but the caretaker is being overly nice and over-giving; that's covert.

When I was eighteen, I went into psychoanalysis, four days on the couch each week, for four and a half years. My analyst was a very nice person, but psychoanalysts don't say much. I talked; he listened. After four and a half years, he said, "You're analyzed."

I took that to mean I was ready to get married, so I met my husband, and we fell madly in love—

for about three weeks. I spent the next thirty years trying to get that back. I learned a lot, and I'm very grateful for that time, because it created the basis for the work that I do now: Inner Bonding.

At some point, I started to see moments when my husband and I would connect again. I started to look at what was happening when we connected. I saw that when we connected, we were both very open. We were in our hearts. The rest of the time, we weren't.

That's when I created the concept of intention that is the basis of Inner Bonding. At any given moment, there are only two intentions. One is the intention to learn about loving yourself and then sharing your love with others. The other is the intention to protect against pain with various forms of controlling behavior.

I saw that if my husband came to me upset or angry, he was protecting from what we now call the *wounded self.* It's the ego part of us; we call it the *wounded self,* because sometimes *ego* has a bad connotation.

I saw that when my husband came to me in his wounded self, either withdrawn or blaming, I would be triggered into my wounded self. This meant, first of all, that I would feel like a deer in the headlights, because that's what I learned when my mother was mad. I didn't know what to do, but I would try to fix it. I would apologize even if I didn't know what I had done. I would try to do anything I could to make things better.

Of course, I was training my husband to treat me badly, because I was treating myself badly. For a long time, I didn't know that.

I discovered this concept of intention about seven years into the marriage, and that's when we wrote our best-selling book. (He was also a psychologist.) The book, *Do I Have to Give Up Me to Be Loved by You?*, has sold over a million copies around the world, but during the seven years it took to write the book, we fought almost the whole time. People would write us, saying, "Your marriage sounds like ours, but how do you stay open to learning in the face of fear?" I didn't know the answer. When anybody got upset with me or yelled at me, I had so much fear that I couldn't stay open to learning. I had no idea how to do that.

I had already become a psychotherapist and practiced traditional therapy for seventeen years; I had also gone into many different kinds of therapy after psychoanalysis, but I was not at all happy with the results for both myself and my clients. I wasn't happy; the marriage wasn't happy.

Always looking at what *I* needed to do, I thought it was all my fault: What do I need to change? How do I need to do things better? But I wasn't finding the answers in all these different forms of therapy.

Let me go back a little bit. My grandmother was an Orthodox Jew, and her God was very punishing and judgmental. My parents were atheists, they had no belief system, and they were always fighting for my allegiance. I looked at both of them and said, "Uh-uh." I didn't see that what either of them believed was making them happy.

At some point in my early twenties, I got onto a spiritual path, I got a guru, and I joined a meditation group, along with doing traditional psychotherapy. Nothing was really working.

So, after practicing traditional psychotherapy with my clients for seventeen years, I started to pray for a process that would work fast and deep, and which people could learn and use on their own so they didn't have to keep going to a therapist every time something happened that they couldn't handle. I knew there must be something.

That's when I met Dr. Erika Chopich, the co-creator of Inner Bonding. Of course, we had to meet, because she had half the process, and I had the other half. She had grown up in a very difficult environment, and she knew from the time that she was young that she had an inner child that she had to take care of. I didn't know that, because I was so externally oriented.

After Erika and I met, Spirit brought in the Inner Bonding process. Over a number of years, it evolved into a very powerful six-step process, which is the subject of this book.

This book is like a first piano lesson: you are going to learn Inner Bonding, but as with any process, like learning to play the piano, you have to practice; you don't just get it at once. You're going to be learning the steps of Inner Bonding, and I hope you take this tool with you and bring it into your life, because it is truly life changing.

After I started to practice Inner Bonding, my whole life changed. At that time, I did not have good health, but soon after I started to learn how to love myself, I became extraordinarily healthy, and I found joy for the first time in my life.

I had been a sickly child, and I hated being sick. In my early twenties, I started to read about what creates health. Fortunately, I read a book called *The Poisons in Your Foods*, by William F. Longgood, as well as *Silent Spring* by Rachel Carson, and I knew they were right. I threw everything out of my kitchen. At that time there was one little health food store in Los Angeles, where I was living, and that's where

I shopped. I started eating only organic food when I was twenty-two years old. That was sixty years ago, and I'm now eighty-two; all this time I've been eating organic foods. I feel very fortunate to have found out about this long ago. Currently, my health is extraordinary. My energy is extraordinary.

But when Inner Bonding came in, I wasn't healthy, and I didn't know why. At that time I didn't know it was because I was abandoning myself rather than loving myself.

When I met Erika, I found out that although she came from a scientific background, she had the ability to look at you and see your aura; she could see the colors. She thought everybody could do that. She didn't know that that was a special gift. When she found out, she called things like that "hooey-wooey," and she didn't want to have anything to do with hooey-wooey stuff.

As we started to create Inner Bonding, we realized that a major part of doing this process is being loving to yourself. We didn't know how to do that. She didn't learn it in her family, and I didn't learn it in mine. We barely knew what love was. How do you find out what love is when you grow up in a family that is not loving?

I realized that I needed to access a higher source of information about love. What was loving to me, and what was loving to others? I had been trying to do this. I had been listening to tapes about opening the channel. I was with a guru, and I was trying hard to connect to a source of guidance. Every once in a while, I would feel something, but it was just accidental; I didn't know how to make it happen. I didn't know how to have divine connection at will, and I wanted that. When I met Erika and we started to develop Inner Bonding, I realized that what I had learned about intention had to do with other people. I didn't realize that it was about really learning about myself and taking loving care of myself.

At one point, Erika, who had lived in Los Angeles, moved to Santa Fe. One day she called me up in the morning, and said, "Oh my God, you will never believe what happened last night."

"What?"

"I got in bed, and there was an old Indian lady at the foot of my bed. I thought she was a homeless person, and I said, 'Who are you, and why are you in my bedroom?' She said, 'I am your spiritual master teacher, and I have come to teach you.'"

"Oh, my God!" I said. "That's what we've been hoping for. What did you do?"

"I told her to leave me alone and go haunt you. I don't want this hooey-wooey stuff."

The woman kept coming back, and finally Erika accepted her; in fact, she had known her as a child. This woman had helped her through a very rough childhood, so she started to be able to have contact with her.

One day Erika came home from the market and said, "Oh, my God! I was in the market. It was so crowded. I could see everybody's teachers, and I could see all their power animals flying around."

Erika was overwhelmed by this experience; she didn't know how to handle it. For my part, I started getting jealous. I wanted to have this happen for me.

One evening, I was lying in bed; I wasn't feeling very well. I was wearing a pink sweat outfit, and I was talking to Erika on the phone. I said, "You're seeing other people's teachers, so maybe you can see mine."

"Well, I'll try."

There was silence on the phone, and all of a sudden Erika said, "Whoa. This is weird. I'm in my house, but I think I'm also in your house. Are you lying in your bed wearing a pink sweat outfit?" (Talk about hooey-wooey!) "Your teacher is working on your body."

Erika introduced me to this being, and then I realized I had seen her. I am an artist, and I paint, and I had seen her at times when I was painting. I asked Erika, "How do I have contact? How do I connect with her?"

"Tonight, get in the bathtub, and imagine that you are painting. Get into that creative state."

So I did. I got into that creative state and started asking questions, and answers started coming. It was amazing!

The next morning, I asked Erika, "Do I have to be in the bathtub to do this?"

"No, it's the state you're in."

Then I realized that the state she was talking about was the state I'm in when my intention is to learn. As I diligently practiced being open to learning—about my own feelings, about what love is and about what was loving to me, I started to have this access quite easily.

I got excited and thought, "Wow! I'm going to help my clients to have this access to their spiritual guidance."

Except it didn't work that way. I'd thought if they just opened to learning, they would have access to higher knowledge. Why wasn't it happening? It took me a while to connect the dots and realize it's about raising your frequency.

The intention to learn raises your frequency, which we need to do to access our higher guidance because Spirit exists at a higher frequency than we do. Our mind needs to be at a high frequency, which happens when we are open to learning about loving ourselves, but our bodies have to be at a higher frequency as well. Mine was, because I had been eating organic food all that time. But most people are eating fast food or food contaminated with pesticides. They're eating foods with genetically modified organisms (GMOs); they're eating processed, packaged foods with sugar and processed oils. All of these lower the frequency of the body, often making it very hard to connect with higher learning, even if somebody is truly open to it. If their body is in a low frequency, it's going to make it a lot harder for them to connect with their higher guidance.

I finally grasped that it takes these two things, which I wrote about in my book *Diet for Divine Connection*: eating really cleanly, to keep the frequency of your body high, and being open to learning about loving yourself. When you do those two things, you will be amazed at how easily you start to connect with your higher guidance.

This is very specific. It's not just about being loving in the world: that comes later. It has to start with what's loving to you, because if you're not loving yourself, if you're just going out into the world to try to love others, you will have an agenda to get love from other people. You will be giving to get love, which is controlling.

That was an amazing realization for me. That's a lot about what I'm going to be discussing.

2

Beyond the Wounded Self

There are many different terms for what I call the *core self*: your true self, your essence, your soul, your inner child. I will use these terms interchangeably, because they all point to the beautiful spark of the Divine that is who we really are. This is our soul. This is the immortal part of us. We are not our lower left brain, the left aspect of the amygdala, which is the location of the wounded self. We are not what that programmed part of us thinks we are. We are a part of what you could call God, Spirit, Divine, or the Universe. We all have that inside of us, which is a powerful source of inner guidance. This is the part of our soul that is in our body, but the energy of our soul is very big, and can't all fit inside our body, so the rest of our soul is all around us. This is our higher guidance.

We call the part of our soul that is in our body the *inner child,* because we need to take responsibility for it, like a child, although we don't always remember that fact. This part of us often communicates through feelings. Our feelings are an incredible source of guidance: they have an enormous amount of information for us.

The inner child is our true self, and it wants to express who we are. It wants learn more about loving, to continue to evolve as a loving human being, and express the gifts that we've been given. We came in expecting to be seen and loved, but unfortunately many of us were not, because if your parents didn't know who they were inside, they couldn't see who you were.

In many cases, our parents projected their woundedness, their not-good-enough feelings about themselves, onto us. We absorbed those projections, so the basis of the wounded self is, "I'm not good enough. I'm not enough. I'll never be enough. I'm flawed. I'm inadequate."

The wounded self is the part of us that was programmed with false beliefs about ourselves—about what we can and can't control, about other people, about Spirit. Many of us operate from these beliefs without realizing that we are being controlled and limited by them. These beliefs are absorbed into the lower part of the left brain called the amygdala. This is where the fight-or-flight mechanism is. It's the false beliefs of our wounded self that triggers fear, even when there is no current real and present danger.

The wounded self knows nothing about love or truth. Nevertheless, it thinks it's the voice of knowledge. It's got a loud voice, and it says, "You're no good." "Who do you think you are?" "You're a loser." "You're going to end up on the streets." "If you act this way, people will like you, and if you're perfect, people will like you, and then you'll be OK." This voice is very loud and demanding, whereas the voice of Spirit is often quite soft.

One way to know the difference between the voice of your wounded self and the voice of your higher guidance is that the voice of the wounded self creates anxiety, depression, guilt, shame, anger, aloneness, emptiness, and jealousy. These are called the wounded feelings, because we create them from how we treat ourselves and what we tell ourselves from our wounded self.

This part of the self can be of many different emotional ages, depending on when we learned and absorbed particular a belief, addiction, or protection against pain. If you started smoking when you were twelve, then, when you smoke, you are operating out of your twelve-year-old. If you started drinking at fifteen, then when you are drinking, you are operating out of your fifteen-year-old. If you learned to be a good girl or boy when you were two or three, when you are doing this, you are operating out of that young place. The wounded self has many ages, all the way through adolescence into early adulthood. We can be these different ages at different times, depending on what is triggered. Maybe you learned to have tantrums when you were very small, and that's your go-to when you're scared or threatened: you get angry and you try and control with anger.

We all have a wounded self, and Inner Bonding is partly about healing its false beliefs. The more you heal the beliefs and operate out of truth, the happier, the lighter, the freer and more joyful you are. That's what emotional freedom is: operating out of truth, not out of the false beliefs of the wounded self.

As we go through the process of Inner Bonding, you will see that when we are upset, we can see where the pain is coming from and the programmed false beliefs that we are usually unaware of. It's not that hard to become aware of these beliefs, but it does take time. It's a layering process.

The next part of ourselves I want to describe is the *loving adult*. The loving adult is like the emissary between Spirit and child. Imagine that with one hand you are holding the hand of God or Spirit or Universe, and with the other hand you are holding the hand of your inner child. You're the one that takes action, because Spirit can't take action. Spirit is spirit: it can't take any action. *We* can take action. We are being loving adults when our intention is to learn about loving ourselves and we are connected with our higher source of love and truth.

Here is why intention is so important: the moment we choose the intention to protect against pain with some form of controlling behavior, we go right into the wounded self. Our intention activates the wounded self. But the moment our true intention is to learn to love ourselves so we can eventually share love with others, that's when we become loving adults. This process takes place moment by moment.

It's not like, "OK, I'm going to be open from now on." It takes a lot of practice, because the wounded self is our default setting. It's what we've all learned to do. It's the automatic, unconscious place we go to as soon as we're scared or threatened or hurt. That's what needs healing, and it's what is healed as you learn and practice the Inner Bonding process, develop your loving adult, and learn to take loving actions based on the truth rather than on the false beliefs of your wounded self.

There are two paths in life. There is the earthly path of fear, which is the path of the wounded self. There is the spiritual path of love and courage, which is the path of the loving adult. We are beings of free will. We can choose who we want to be at any given moment. We can choose to try and control in the face of fear, or to open to learning about what is loving to ourselves and others, even in the face of fear. Fear does not have to determine what we do.

This is a scary planet, especially now, but that doesn't mean that we have to be its victims. We can choose to be loving even in the face of fear, but it has to be a conscious choice.

The whole purpose of the wounded self is to get love and avoid pain in order to feel safe. By contrast, the purpose of the loving adult is to learn to love ourselves and share that love with others. It's a completely different purpose. One is to *get* love. The other is to *be* love and share love. The wounded self desires to find happiness, safety, lovability, and worth externally, through people, things, activities, and substances. The wounded self thinks, "Am I OK? Do you like me? Am I doing a good job? You have to like me, or I'm not OK." The wounded self is externally oriented. It makes other people responsible for whether or not we are OK. But once we hand this responsibility to someone else, we have to try to control them.

The loving adult desires to find joy, peace, safety, lovability, and worth internally, by connecting with our higher source of love and truth and bringing it down into us. It's about learning to fill ourselves with love so that we truly have love to share. If we are always out there trying to get love, there is an emptiness inside. When we are not learning to bring love inside and love ourselves, we are empty, and we don't have any love to share when we are empty. That's why we are trying to get love. Once you truly learn to love yourself and bring love inside, you feel full of love, and you have a deep desire to share that love with others.

Again, the intention of the wounded self is to protect against pain and avoid responsibility for feeling it, while the intent of the loving adult is to learn to love and take responsibility for our own pain, our own joy, for all of our own feelings. The wounded self always wants to *get rid of feelings* rather than learning from them. Taking responsibility means wanting to know what we're doing to cause the feelings.

There are two kinds of negative feelings. The first kind is wounded feelings, such as anxiety, depression, guilt, shame, anger, aloneness, emptiness, and jealousy. We cause these feelings with the various ways we abandon ourselves, such as judging ourselves, ignoring our feelings, numbing our feelings with various addictions, and making others responsible for our feelings of worth and safety.

Then there are the core painful feelings of life, what I call the existential feelings, such as loneliness, heartbreak, grief, helplessness over other people, and sorrow. These are caused by other people or events. Although we are not responsible for the fact that people or events are causing these feelings in us, we are still responsible for lovingly managing these feelings with compassion towards ourselves.

We affect one another. We can cause one another pain, and we are responsible for that. But I can also take responsibility for being compassionate if somebody is being unloving to me. I can take responsibility if I have hurt somebody. We are not islands. We affect one another.

Either our heart is closed or its open. This is automatic, depending on your intent When your intention is to control, to protect, to avoid pain, your heart closes; the whole chakra system closes. We clamp down. When our intention is to learn about loving ourselves, we open. Everything becomes expansive. Consequently, you can start to tell what your intention is by how you're feeling. If you're feeling closed up and constricted inside, you know that your intention is to control. If you're feeling free and expansiveness, you know that your intention is to learn about love and truth.

Here are some of the addictive ways people avoid their feelings. Be aware that whether or not these choices are addictive and avoidant depend on your intent. You can watch TV to enjoy your favorite program, or you can surf the channels to avoid your feelings. You can meditate to connect with your guidance, or to bliss out and avoid responsibility for your feelings. You can read because you love to read or learn, or you can read to avoid your feelings.

I would like you to take out a pen or pencil and mark on this list what you do when you are triggered into your wounded self. Please, no judgment. If you judge yourself for any of these—and judgment is a major form of control—it will shut you down. We cannot learn when we judge. Please don't judge. We all do these things. We've all learned to do these things. We are not bad or wrong for doing them. It's just that this is what we learned to do as we were growing up to avoid our feelings because when we were young we couldn't handle our painful feelings.

- TV
- Compulsive thinking, ruminating
- Work
- Withdrawal
- Reading
- Getting sick
- Sports
- Being critical of self or others
- Anorexia
- Denial
- Exercise
- Smiling, laughing, or joking
- Power over others
- Compliance with others' demands
- Gambling
- Being a packrat
- Accumulating money
- Accumulating information
- Spending
- Fantasizing, daydreaming
- Sleep
- Shopping
- Shoplifting
- Anger or irritation
- Fighting
- Worry
- Misery, depression
- Meditation
- Talking on the phone
- Drama
- Over-talking with endless details
- Beautifying
- Danger
- Busywork
- Computer
- The Internet
- Religion
- Crime
- Pushing to accomplish things
- Masturbation
- Pornography
- Time urgency
- Gossiping

- Adrenaline and other stress hormones
- Self-mutilation: cutting, nail-biting, picking on skin

The wounded self doesn't want to be unmasked. It doesn't want you to know that you're doing these things to control or avoid or protect. If you start to feel uncomfortable inside, realize it's your wounded self going into denial and saying, "No, no, no! I don't do those things."

While these choices might work temporarily to numb out your pain, which is how they became addictions, what actually happens that your fear increases, and you feel more unsafe and insecure. The wounded self does these things to try to feel safe, but in the longer term they make you feel more unsafe and more insecure. It's like if a child comes to you upset, and you just give the child a cookie and say, "Go watch TV," it pacifies the child for the moment, but does not deal with whatever is going on. That's what happens when we shove our emotional issues down by turning to addictive and controlling behaviors. You might eat the sugar, have the drink or cigarette, or yell at somebody; it feels better for the moment, but you haven't handled the issue, so you eventually feel more unsafe and more insecure.

Signs of Feeling Unsafe and Insecure

Within Self

• Sad, depressed, alone inside, lonely

• Victimized, powerless, helpless, fearful, anxious, desperate

• Empty, numb, hopeless, unfulfilled, purposeless

• Angry, hurt, jealous, envious, insecure, untrusting

• Ashamed, guilty, unlovable, unworthy

• Trapped, stuck, going in circles

In Relationships

• Codependent: taker/caretaker system, dependent

• Disconnected, distant, unsupportive

• Conflicted, angry, blaming, locked into power struggles

• Violent, violating, disrespectful

• Nonsexual, unable to give or receive love

• Dishonest, suspicious, undermining

There is no way around these results. There is no way around these consequences. When we are operating out of our wounded self, this is how we are going to feel. This is always going to be the result.

There is another reason for some of the feelings, like anxiety and depression: eating badly, eating sugar and processed industrial seed oils like safflower and sunflower oil, which are not natural. You're eating processed, devitalized foods, you're eating foods that have been genetically modified and sprayed with pesticides like Roundup (aka glyphosate), and you've got these chemicals in your system. They destroy the balance in the gut, resulting in what's called *gut dysbiosis*. Our gut is the center of about 80–85 percent of our immune system. We have a whole breed of beings living in there that keep us alive. Antibiotics, drugs, and poor-quality food disrupt the balance in our system, and the bad bacteria take over and proliferate. When they do, they cause the lining of the gut to loosen up. It's supposed to stay tight, so food can't get into it, but when the lining loosens up (called *leaky gut syndrome*), food particles get in, which affects the organs. In fact, researchers are finding that this is a major cause of cancer, heart disease, autoimmune disease, diabetes, Alzheimer's, Parkinson's, even autism. These degenerative diseases have been proliferating because of a huge imbalance in the gut that is caused by food and medications. These bad bacteria are very toxic. They go up the vagus nerve into the brain, creating anxiety and depression.

In the past, if somebody got depressed, it was mainly from unresolved childhood issues or from how they were treating themselves. But now it's also from our food supply, which is very sad. In fact, I want to recommend a documentary called *Secret Ingredients*. It will show you what is really happening with our food supply and why there is so much illness.

3

The Inner Bonding Process

In this chapter, I'm going to briefly go through the Inner Bonding process. I hope you will turn to it instead of automatically going to protective, controlling behaviors. With practice, you are going to learn to turn to the six steps of Inner Bonding any time you feel anything other than peace inside.

The Six Steps of Inner Bonding

1. Be willing to feel pain and/or fear, and take responsibility for your feelings and security.

2. Choose the intent to learn about love and fear. Invite Spirit into your heart. Open your heart to compassion, becoming a loving adult.

3. Welcome and dialogue with wounded selves, exploring fears, false beliefs, memories, and

resulting behavior that is causing the pain.
Explore gifts and what brings joy to your core self.

4. Dialogue with spiritual guidance, exploring truth and loving action toward your inner child.

5. Take loving action. Put God into motion.

6. Evaluate the effectiveness of your actions.

1. Be willing to feel pain and/or fear, and take responsibility for your feelings. This means being aware and being present in your body. Most of us have learned to stay in our heads. We've learned to disconnect and disassociate from our bodies and our feelings because we couldn't manage them; we couldn't manage the pain of childhood. As a result, we've learned to stay up in the head, which is a form of self-abandonment. When we were little, it may have saved our lives to disconnect, but now we need to learn to get back into our bodies. If you don't know what you feel, how can you attend to it? Our feelings have a great deal of vital information for us. Once you realize that, you won't avoid that information; you're going to want those feelings.

Step 1 is moving into being present in the body, being aware of what you feel. I call it "having your inner baby monitor on." If you have a baby and you want to be a loving parent, you don't just put the baby to sleep and go out to lunch. You've got a baby monitor on, and the minute that baby wakes up and cries, you are there. The baby's cry is information. It's saying, "I'm hungry," "I'm wet," "I'm scared," "I feel alone."

When we feel anything less than inner peace, our inner child is giving us information, and we need to learn to attend to it as a loving adult. It took me a long time to be in my body, because as I've said, I was very externally oriented. It took me a long time to learn to become present. Now, because I'm present in my body, I attend to my feelings the second there is anything other than peace going on inside.

2. Move into the intent to learn. Learn to move into your heart, which is the seat of the loving adult. Consciously open to learning. Invite the love, compassion, truth, wisdom, and kindness of Spirit into your heart so that you will become a loving adult. If there is something less than peace with your inner child, you need to be a loving adult to attend to it. In step 2, we choose to be a loving adult. We open to learning, and we invite in the compassion and the love of Spirit into our heart.

3. Inner dialogue with your inner child and your wounded self. Let's say you realize that you are feeling anxious. You say to the part that's anxious, "What am I telling you? How am I treating you? What am I doing or not doing that's causing you to feel this way?" This is about learning to take responsibility for our feelings.

Suppose the inner child says, "You are putting pressure on me. You're telling me that I've got to do this perfectly. I can't make a mistake, or you're not going to love me. I'm not going to be OK unless this or that person gives me approval. So of course I feel anxious."

It's like telling a child before going to a party that they have to do and say everything right. The child's going to be a wreck. That's what happens at the inner level when we put this much pressure on ourselves. When we judge and put pressure on ourselves, we create anxiety, depression, guilt, shame, and many other negative feelings.

Once you understand that you're feeling anxious (or any other wounded feeling) because you're telling yourself you've got to be perfect, you go a little deeper, to the wounded self. A common false belief of the wounded self is that if you're perfect, you'll have control over getting the approval and the love you need, and you'll be OK.

We want to go down to the level of the wounded self in order to see where we learned that belief. Why do we continue to think that we can control how people feel about us by being perfect, saying the right thing, looking right, making a certain amount of money, or having a certain kind of job or car or house? Why do we continue to believe that when it creates anxiety? We are taking a look at the beliefs that we've been operating from without realizing it.

Once we have a full picture of what we are telling ourselves, we go to step 4.

4. Dialogue with your divine guidance. Step 4 is basically asking two questions: *what is the truth about these false beliefs that I've uncovered?* and *what would be loving to myself?*

The loving adult does not know the answers. As a loving adult, I don't have any answers. That's why I have to learn to go to my higher self, to my guidance, for everything, because I was not brought up in an environment where I saw what it means to be loving. The good thing is, we don't have to know, because our higher guidance knows. When you learn to access it, that's where the answers are.

As a loving adult, I'm the one that takes the action based on that guidance, but I myself don't know. I've come to believe that I don't know any-thing. But I don't have to know, because the guidance is there, in my higher self.

Let's say that I've come upon the belief that if I were perfect, I would be OK and get love. I say to Spirit, "Well, is that true?" When you really get connected, Spirit might say, "What you think is perfect somebody else might not think is perfect at all. So what does 'perfect' mean? Second, can somebody control how you feel about them, or do you just decide for yourself? What makes you feel you can control how other people feel about you?"

We are going to get information about what's true and then about what's loving. Spirit might say that you need to become aware of when you're being judgmental, and you need to move into compassion for your feelings, for who you are. That would be a loving action. There are thousands of loving actions, depending on the issues. This is just one example.

5. Take the loving action(s) learned in step 4. Examples:
• Set loving boundaries within self and with others.
• Care for the body, the house of the soul.
• Pursue the calling of the soul.
• Create balance between work and play.
• Spend time holding and being held by your inner child.

- Help others; do service; give to others.
- Practice mindfulness.
- Choose the intent to learn each moment with self and others.
- Practice the six steps throughout the day.
- Make amends.
- Define your own worth and lovability daily.
- Reach out for help when it is needed.

6. Evaluate your actions. This means going back in to see how you feel as a result of taking this loving action. What are you feeling and experiencing? If healing is not occurring, go back to step 4 to discover another loving action. Evidence of healing of the wounded self and release of the core self could include feelings of:

- Personal power
- Self-esteem
- Peace, serenity
- Joy, laughter
- Gratitude
- Freedom
- Integration
- Authenticity
- Transparency
- Playfulness
- Spontaneity
- Connection
- Wisdom
- Knowing
- Intuition
- Vision
- Oneness with Spirit
- Oneness with others
- Compassion
- Love
- Understanding
- Gentleness, kindness

- Trust
- Integrity
- Intimacy
- Conflict resolution
- Respectful
- Truthfulness
- Honoring of self and others

If indeed you've taken a loving action, you are going to feel relief quickly. That's how you know you've done it. It's amazing how good it feels when you take a loving action for yourself.

As you master the six steps and operate more and more as a loving adult, you'll start to feel more safe and secure.

Questioner: What if I ask Spirit, and it doesn't give me the answer? How will I know that it's going to answer me?

Margaret: Actually, Spirit will always answer when you are open to learning. We live in a sea of information. It's been scientifically proven, and I can point you to the books where you can learn about it, such as Dr. Bruce Lipton's book *The Biology of Belief.* Information is always here for us when we operate from a frequency that is high enough. If you're not getting answers, then you need to look to your frequency. Either your body or your thinking is keeping your frequency low.

I've been doing this practice for so long that Spirit is right here and now for me. I didn't grow up with any spiritual belief, so when I started practicing Inner Bonding, I thought I was making it up: "How can it be real? Spirit is there for some people, but not for me."

It's scary to think that you might not get answers, and when you do, at first you don't know where they're coming from. For a long time, I had to do a lot of testing. I would get an answer, and I would follow it and see what happened. Then I would get an answer, didn't follow it, and see what happened. Over time, I realized that I was getting real answers, and they were making a huge difference in my life.

Questioner: I want to share something about parenting. You do need to control children in a sense, because they're still learning, so how can we still be present for them without causing them pain?

Margaret: It's a very good question. Half of parenting is being there for your kids, and the other half is role modeling: being there for yourself by taking responsibility for yourself. That's a great gift to offer kids.

We do need to control certain things with kids: for example, they can't run in the street. But there are so many things that parents try to control that they can't, and in trying to control their children, they are teaching their children to control. Furthermore, in many ways, parents don't take care of themselves, so they are not role-modeling personal responsibility. Would you be willing to come up and do a little work with me on this?

Questioner: Sure.

Margaret: Can you give me an example of an area where you feel you have to control a child?

Questioner: My daughter is about five and a half. At school, she tends to not be very supportive with her friends. She might suggest things to play, and they might say, "I don't want to play that," and she gets upset. Or they might suggest something to play with them. She is not interested, and she says, "I don't want to play that." She then plays by herself, and she's upset and sulking. I have been trying to coach her about being a good sport. If someone doesn't want to play your game, ask them, "What do you want to play?" or something like that.

Margaret: Children can actually learn Inner Bonding fairly easily. What if your child comes to you when she's upset and sulking? What if you said, "What are you telling yourself that's making you feel bad?" Then she becomes aware of what she is telling herself. Something is going on inside her; possibly she is telling herself, "I'm not good enough" or "Nobody likes me." Where did she get that? Instead of trying to control her feelings, you can help her to learn from them.

Children generally don't need a lot of control. They need role modeling more than anything. When I was living in L.A., an elementary school was teaching the kids Inner Bonding. They called it "Tune In, Tune Up." One teacher told me about a situation where a seven-year-old girl was struggling with reading, and she was really upset about it. The teacher came over and said, "Honey, what's wrong?"

The child said, "I am having such a hard time."

"Why don't you do Tune In, Tune Up?"

Pretty soon her little face brightened up. The teacher came over and said, "It looks like you are getting some help."

The little girl said, "Oh, yes. My guidance told me that I'm feeling bad because I'm judging myself, and it's a lot easier to stop judging myself than it is to learn to read." If a seven-year-old can learn to do that, we can too!

Questioner: In close relationships, could one person be operating from the wounded self while the other is operating from the loving adult? Is it possible that at some point, because of the way the relationship goes, the loving adult may revert back to the wounded self?

Margaret: People come together at their common level of woundedness or health. It's not always easy to see one's own forms of protection. If somebody is truly coming from a loving adult state, they are not going to be attracted to somebody who is in their wounded self.

That's why I suggest that if you're single and want to find a partner, you do your inner work to learn to be a loving adult. Then you're going to attract somebody who is also coming more from their loving adult, or at least is open to learning.

People commonly come together in woundedness or health at any age. In my marriage, we came together at our common level of woundedness. But I was always searching, looking, learning, and growing. When Inner Bonding came in and I started to practice it, I moved into a completely different state, but my husband never did open to learning. I moved on from the relationship because there was no way to connect when you are in two completely different places.

Questioner: Is it better to be operating from the core self or from the loving adult?

Margaret: When you are operating as a loving adult, you are including your core self. You're nurturing, you're loving, you're allowing your essence to express. We appear to separate out this part so that we can do the healing, but as you develop your loving adult, you access your core self, your guidance; you're taking loving action. It's a smooth integration; there's not a sense of separation anymore. Really that's the goal: a sense of oneness, not only with ourselves, but with each other. The more you have that inner sense of oneness, which you will experience as you develop your loving adult, the more you will easily see the essence of others and feel a sense of oneness with them.

That's where we need to go in our culture. In order to get beyond the problems of our society, such as racism and sexism, we need to develop that sense of oneness, but it has to start with ourselves.

Margaret: At this point, I'd like to take someone through an Inner Bonding process. What's your name?

Wendy: Wendy.

Margaret: I would like you to start taking some deep breaths. As you breathe, put your mind on your breath, and let your breath take you down inside your body, out of your thinking mind, out of your programmed mind. As you breathe, scan your body for any physical sensations. What do you notice physically in your body right now?

Wendy: A vibration in my neck.

Margaret: Breathe into that, please. Become present with it. Imagine that it's your inner child giving you a message by creating a vibration in your neck. Just sit with that little girl for a moment. Now breathe into your heart, and open to learning about what you might be telling yourself or how you're treating yourself that's causing this feeling. Invite the presence of love and compassion into your heart. This is step 2 of Inner Bonding, and this is how we become a loving adult. Do you have a spiritual connection?

Wendy: I do have faith, yes.

Margaret: Is there anything in particular that you open to?

Wendy: I open to God.

Margaret: I want you to invite the presence of God into your heart—the presence of love, the presence of compassion, into your heart. Is God love and compassion for you?

Wendy: Yes.

Margaret: Now I would like you to ask your little girl, "Is there something I'm telling you or some way I'm treating you right now that's making my neck vibrate?" Just ask the question in your mind. Go inside to the place in your neck that's vibrating, and let the answer come from there. It doesn't have to be right. You don't have to put any pressure on it, but what does that vibration want to say to you?

Wendy: I've been trying to get here, but this is where I'm lacking.

Margaret: There is some pain going on right now, isn't there?

Wendy: Yes.

Margaret: I want you to breathe into the pain. Where do you feel the pain in your body, Wendy?

Wendy: My neck.

Margaret: So there is pain in there, right?

Wendy: Yes.

Margaret: So your little girl is hurting. The way she is showing you that she is in pain is by making your neck vibrate, right? Just breathe into that pain. Don't try to make it go away. Don't do anything to get rid of it. Ask your little girl, "How am I treating you? What am I telling you? What am I doing or not doing that's causing you this pain?"

Wendy: I am not being truthful to myself.

Margaret: How are you not being truthful to yourself? What does that mean?

Wendy: I haven't been my authentic self.

Margaret: You are not being your authentic self. How are you stopping yourself from being your authentic self?

Wendy: I take on the other person. I do what they need, what they want. I take on their likes.

Margaret: So your little girl is hurting because you are making other people's feelings more important than hers? That's hurting her, isn't it?

Wendy: Yes.

Margaret: Let's go a little deeper. How old were you when you started doing that?

Wendy: I started smoking at thirteen, but at about four years old.

Margaret: What was happening at four?

Wendy: I lost my grandfather, and he was very important to me. I had a dysfunctional family. I had two brothers who were alcoholics, into drugs. There was a lot of attention paid to that. I was a good kid.

Margaret: So you learned to be a good kid as part of your survival strategy? You learned to take care of all these things that were going on around you just to be OK, right?

Wendy: Just not to cause any trouble.

Margaret: But now the problem is, you are still doing that, right?

Wendy: Yes.

Margaret: See if you can go into the part of you that is still doing that and ask, "What do you hope for by taking care of everybody else, by taking responsibility for everybody else's feelings?"

Wendy: I just want to be loved.

Margaret: Right. So that little four-year-old thinks that if you take care of everybody else's feelings, they will love you. What is actually happening? It's not working, is it?

Wendy: No.

Margaret: Let's go to God right now. Ask if it is true that the only way to be loved is to take care of everybody else. You learned long ago to try to take care of everybody else to get love, but in doing that, you are abandoning your little girl, and she is feeling unloved by you. That's why she is hurting. She is feeling rejected by you.

Wendy: I don't know how to love her.

Margaret: Right. You don't know how to love her. You know how to take care of everybody else, but you don't know how to love her.

Wendy: I don't think she's good. I tell myself all the time that I'm not good enough.

Margaret: OK, so there is one of the false beliefs: "I'm not good enough." I want you to ask God if there is any way it could be true that who you are in your soul is not good enough.

Wendy: He thinks I am good enough.

Margaret: Yes. Whom are you going to believe? Are you going to believe your four-year-old wounded self, who decided you weren't good enough, or are you going to believe God?

Wendy: I am going to believe God.

Margaret: OK, good. Now ask God, "What is the first thing that I need to do for my little girl so she can start to feel my love for her? What would be the one thing?"

Wendy: I don't know.

Margaret: Do you have children?

Wendy: Yes.

Margaret: Do you have a little girl?

Wendy: She's twenty-three.

Margaret: When she was little and she came to you hurting, what would you do?

Wendy: I would hug her.

Margaret: The first thing is to get yourself a doll or stuffed animal and hug her, just as you would do with a child. Hug her, and let her know that she is not alone. Isn't that what you do with your kids? You let them know you're there, right? You know how to do that, right?

Wendy: I hope I do.

Margaret: I can see that you do.

Wendy: I didn't want to leave the same imprints on them.

Margaret: I don't think you did. But your inner child needs the same thing that you gave your kids. She needs you to hug her and let her know you're there, that she's not alone, and that she's good. How about starting with that?

Wendy: Thank you.

Margaret: How do you feel right now?

Wendy: Good. A little confused. This is what I didn't understand when reading your book, and this is making it easier.

Margaret: I think your little girl does feel some relief, right?

Wendy: Yes.

Margaret: That lets you know you are on the right track. Thank you so much, Wendy. You are very brave.

We've just gone through the Inner Bonding process. In step 1, I had her breathe in, and she tuned into the vibration in her neck.

In step 2, I had Wendy choose the intention to learn and access the love of God and then go in. It takes time before you really get to what is happening, but she did. Her little girl is hurting because she is abandoning her. She is making other people more important. She is telling her she is not good enough. These are all ways we learned to treat ourselves that make us feel bad.

Then we went to Spirit and asked the truth. God said, "No, you are good." We can all see she is good. Her wounded self doesn't know it, but I can see it right away in her. It's not always easy to access the loving action, but if you think about what you would do with a child, it's easier to understand what to do for yourself.

Wendy: When you brought up my daughter, it connected. That love I have for my daughter—if I could give that back to myself! I never made that connection.

Margaret: That's right. Most people know what they would do with a child. That's what you do with yourself. It's no different.

At this point, let me go through the four major ways that we tend to abandon ourselves:

1. We stay up in our head. We've learned to stay in our head as a way of protecting against pain. That's why step 1 is getting into your body.
2. We judge ourselves, which is what you saw here: "You are not good enough." That's one of

the major judgments, but there are many others that we make against ourselves.

3. We turn to addictions to numb out our feelings. Wendy said she was thirteen when she started to smoke. Nobody ever taught her how to handle her feelings. She didn't see that role-modeled. There was chaos in her house. She learned to turn to cigarettes and probably other addictions.

4. We make others responsible for whether or not we are OK. This is what Wendy learned in being a good girl: "I am a good girl, so other people will like me, and then I will be OK."

Almost everybody uses these four ways of self-abandonment in one way or another; I haven't met anybody who doesn't. Everybody has learned to stay in their head, to judge themselves, to turn to addictions, and to make other people responsible for their sense of worth.

In step 1 of Inner Bonding, you want to become aware of your feelings, because any time you do any of these things, you are creating wounded feelings. You're creating the pain, the anxiety, the depression, the guilt, the shame, the anger, the aloneness, the emptiness. All of these wounded feelings are coming mostly from these four ways of abandoning yourself. Can you start to see that?

Questioner: When you were doing your work with Wendy, I was following along, also doing work. It became very clear to me that I want someone else to do it for me. I don't want to eat well; I want you to serve me good food because you love me. I'm not going to eat well until you love me.

Margaret: Yes, that's right. That's a big awareness, isn't it?

Questioner: Earlier you were talking about things that lower the vibration in your body; you mentioned food and thoughts. What are your opinions on music and television? Could visual and audial stimuli also lower that vibration?

Margaret: It depends on what you are watching or listening to. Most of the things on TV are going to lower your frequency. Listening to beautiful music can help raise your frequency.

Many things can help raise your frequency: being in nature, being with animals, listening to music, reading spiritual literature, helping someone else. But to raise your level high enough to access your guidance, the frequency of your body needs to be clear, with a diet of clean, natural food, and you have to be in an intention to learn about loving yourself. That's the key. Once you've made those two choices, other things can support you.

Walking out in nature raises your frequency. Take walks. Practice Inner Bonding out loud. I always recommend that people start with either writing or speaking the process out loud, not in your head. If you are worried about people thinking you are talking to yourself, just put your earbuds in, and they won't know. I live in a rural area, and I go out every morning and do my Inner Bonding out loud. I'm in the country, so people don't see me talking out loud. It's a great way to start the day—to do your Inner Bonding out loud. It sets the tone for the day.

Questioner: Can you share something about what you do in the morning?

Margaret: In the morning, I do prayer. I pray for the people I love. I pray for the people I work with. I pray for the planet. I then move into gratitude, and I'm very thankful for the many blessings that I have. Then I check in and do Inner Bonding. I talk out loud to my little girl. I say, "Hi, sweetie, how are you doing today?" Most of the time she's great, because I have learned to take care of her, but thirty-seven years ago, before I did, I would ask how she was doing, and she'd be really mad at me for abandoning her. Now I say, "How are you doing?" and most of the time I feel peace inside.

When there is nothing for me to attend to inside, I go right to my higher guidance, where I spend a lot of time. It's open-ended for me at this point. I say, "What would you like to say to me? What more can I do? How can I continue to evolve in my ability to love? What would you like to tell me?" I just stay open to what Spirit wants to guide me toward. I always get a lot of information.

Questioner: When you contact your guidance, do you see someone?

Margaret: At this point, I do not. I just open and listen, but for many years, I did visualize. I've had many experiences of having my life saved, and I've tested out Spirit so much that I know 100 percent that Spirit is there. I just ask, and I let it come in.

I do this all day; I don't do anything without asking. The more you do it, the more confident you get that you are never alone. We are always being guided. We have many spirits, or whatever you want to call them, guiding us. I just think of the Universe at this point.

Questioner: I ask myself often, "Why are you feeling anxious?" but often the answer could be,

"I'm feeling anxious because I need to do something in the house, or I need to go to the gym."

Margaret: You are not asking the right question. It's not "Why are you feeling anxious?" It's "What am I telling you? How am I treating you?" If you say, "Why are you feeling anxious?" it's too easy to go to something external, but if you ask, "What am I telling you? Am I telling you you've got to get this done? Am I putting pressure on you?" That's a different question.

Questioner: When you talk about frequency, it makes me think we have to be in some type of alignment. Basically, we are messed up. I am wondering how safe you think it is to get into Inner Bonding. Do you think we need to meditate first, or eat the right foods first, so that we can be at a certain level, or can we just tap right into it? Is it possible that we can feed ourselves the wrong information, so that it's coming from the ego?

Margaret: Your feelings are going to tell you. If you are giving yourself the wrong information, you are not going to feel relief inside. You are going to feel bad. Our feelings are instantly telling us whether we are hearing the truth or lies.

We have two voices inside. We have the voice of love and truth, which is the voice of Spirit, and we've got the voice of fear and lies, which is the voice of the wounded self. It will always lie, because it's programmed with false beliefs, and it has no access to truth. There is no danger, ever, in listening to the voice of love and truth.

Questioner: So it's not just telling me what I want to hear? Because sometimes the truth hurts. In other words, it can't just tell me what I want to hear. Telling me what I want to hear makes me feel good too, even though it's not the right answer.

Margaret: It's not going to make you feel good in the long run if it's not actually true for you. Often what the wounded self does or says feels good in the short term, but in the long term it's not going to give you the relief that you need. When you hear the voice of love and truth, it's a completely different feeling inside. You know that that is what's right for you. It does not hurt. The truth is not going to bring you pain. It's going to free you.

Doing Inner Bonding is going to help you to eat better or help you to do the other things you need to do. The more you see and value and love yourself, the more motivated you are to take care of other things as well.

4

From Lies to Truth

You need to be gentle with yourself in regard to the fact that the wounded self doesn't want to be unmasked. Sometimes that part will just fog out. This was brought home to me one time when I was teaching a workshop, and a young man asked me a question. I answered it, and he looked blank. He said, "Would you mind repeating that?" I repeated it, and he looked blank. He said, "One more time, please." I repeated it. He said, "You know, this must be really important, because I can't hear a word you're saying."

That's what the wounded self does. If you find yourself fogging out during this process, please don't judge yourself. Just gently bring yourself back. Even if you keep leaving, just gently bring yourself back. We do tend to fog out when things hit home.

The wounded self likes to mask as the loving adult. Often people will say the process isn't working. That's because they don't realize that their intention is actually to control. They want to get rid of pain. If your intention is to get rid of pain, you're in your wounded self. *The wounded self always wants to get rid of pain rather than learn from it, take responsibility for it, be compassionate towards it, and understand where it's coming from.*

When you first start the process, it's not always easy to distinguish between the loving adult and the wounded self. Just be aware that the wounded part of us is quite tricky.

The wounded self generally mirrors what happened when we were growing up—how our parents or caregivers treated us, and how they treated themselves. Sometimes parents are very loving towards their children, but completely abandoning with themselves.

I'll frequently get clients who say, "My parents were so loving. They were there for me. I felt so safe." Yet they're completely self-abandoning.

I ask, "How did your parents treat themselves?" It comes to light that their parents were alcoholics, or worked all the time, or were caretakers or martyrs; they completely gave themselves up. It's really important to see the role modeling. We learn from how our caregivers treat themselves even more than from how they treat us.

Take a look at that, and see how you're treating yourself. Is that mirroring what you saw as you were growing up, not just how you were treated?

The wounded self can be any age; often it's a child or adolescent that acts like an adult. When there is no loving adult, it takes on the role of the adult, but it can't be an adult, because it doesn't know how, and it has no access to the guidance of Spirit.

When we're in our wounded self, our frequency is low. It's low any time our intention is to control, avoid, or protect against pain. We can't access the truth or loving action when our frequency is low. Whenever the wounded self is in charge, we are abandoning ourselves. The intention of the wounded self is to protect against pain, to control, to avoid feelings and avoid responsibility for our feelings. The heart closes down, and the child inside feels alone and abandoned.

As I've said, the wounded self is the part of us that has all false beliefs about who we are and how the world is. It's a learned aspect. Although we're born with the instinct of fight-or-flight or freeze, we learn our false beliefs. Because we learned them, we can unlearn them. That's the good news;

that's what healing is. Healing is moving from lies to truth. Healing is moving from what's not real to what's real.

The following lists of false beliefs might be helpful to you in tuning in to the false beliefs that you are currently operating from *now*—not from the past. Check them off from your wounded self, not from the part of you who might know that they are not currently true.

Check the things you may have heard or absorbed from your parents, siblings, teachers, friends, TV, or society and that your child-adult may still believe.

False Beliefs about Happiness and Self-Worth

☐ My adequacy, lovability, and feelings of self-worth and come from others liking me and approving of me.

☐ My sense of happiness and well-being comes from another loving me.

☐ Others' disapproval or rejection mean that I'm not good enough.

☐ I can't make myself happy.

☐ I can't make myself as happy as someone or something else can.

☐ My best feelings come from outside myself, from how others, or a particular other sees me and treats me.

False Beliefs about Responsibility for Feelings

THE CARETAKER POSITION

☐ I'm responsible for others' feelings. Therefore, I should never do anything that hurts or upsets another even, if it's something that makes me happy and is not intended to hurt anyone.

☐ It's up to me to make the people I care about happy.

☐ When others around me are unhappy, it's my fault and/ or my responsibility to do something about it.

☐ If I don't take responsibility for other's happiness and unhappiness, I'm not a caring person.

☐ If I take responsibility for my own happiness instead of putting others first, I'm being selfish.

☐ If other people are angry at me, I make them feel that way, and I'm responsible for fixing their feelings.

☐ It is my responsibility to heal wounded people.

THE TAKER POSITION

☐ Others are responsible for my feelings. Therefore, if someone cares about me, he or she will never do anything that hurts or upsets me.

☐ I can't take care of myself. I need someone to take care of me.

☐ I can't be alone. I feel like I'll die if I'm alone.

☐ When I'm hurt or upset, it's someone else's fault.

☐ It's up to other people to make me feel good about myself by approving of me.

☐ I'm not responsible for my feelings. Other people make me feel happy, sad, angry, frustrated, shut down, or depressed.

☐ When I'm angry, someone makes me feel that way and is responsible for fixing my feelings.

☐ I'm not responsible for my behavior. Other people make me yell, act crazy, get sick, laugh, cry, get violent, leave, or fail.

☐ Others are selfish if they do what they want instead of what I want or need.

☐ If I'm not connected to someone, I will die.

False Beliefs about Pain

☐ I can't handle my pain, especially the pain of disapproval, rejection, abandonment, the pain of being shut out, or the pain of isolation and aloneness.

☐ If I open to my pain, I will fall apart. I will go crazy or die.

☐ If I open to my pain, it will be unending.

☐ Once I start to cry, I'll never stop.

☐ Showing pain is a sign of weakness.

☐ People will think less of me if they see me cry.

☐ If I cry, I will be rejected, or people will think I'm crazy.

☐ No one really wants to hear about my pain.

☐ No one can handle the depth of my pain.

☐ My problems are so trivial compared to other people's that I have no right to be in pain.

☐ Why should I have to feel this pain? I don't deserve it.

☐ There's no point in opening to pain. It doesn't make anything better. "Why cry over spilled milk?"

False Beliefs about the Inner Child and Core Self

☐ I'm basically bad, wrong, or defective.

☐ I'm too intelligent, too smart for my own good.

☐ I don't have a good sense of humor.

☐ I'm immature.

☐ I'm not a professional.

☐ I never went to college.

☐ I didn't graduate from high school.

☐ I have a small vocabulary.

☐ I can't do math.

☐ I don't read well.

☐ I have no imagination.

☐ I'm not spiritual enough.

☐ I'm too spiritual.

☐ I can't do anything right.

☐ I was abused as a child.

☐ When bad things happen, it's always my fault.

☐ Bad things always happen to me.

☐ I have an eating disorder.

☐ I'm an alcoholic.

☐ I'm a drug addict.

☐ I'm too sexual.

☐ I'm a sex addict.

☐ I'm not sexual enough.

- ☐ I'm crazy.
- ☐ I'm a phony.
- ☐ I'm righteous and arrogant.
- ☐ I'm depressed.
- ☐ I'm superficial.
- ☐ I'm screwed up.
- ☐ I'm boring.
- ☐ I have no personality.
- ☐ I'm a goody-goody.
- ☐ I'm a man.
- ☐ I'm a woman.
- ☐ I'm not good enough.
- ☐ I'm not lovable.
- ☐ I'm not adequate.
- ☐ I don't count, don't matter, am unimportant.
- ☐ I'm in the way, a bother, too much trouble.
- ☐ I'm bad, wrong, unworthy, defective, inadequate, unlovable, a bother, unimportant, or not good enough because:
    - ○ I'm too tall.
    - ○ I'm too short.
    - ○ I'm too skinny.
    - ○ I don't make enough money.
    - ○ I don't drive a nice car.
    - ○ I'm a geek, a dork.
    - ○ Nobody likes me.
    - ○ I'm shy.
    - ○ I'm too aggressive.

○ I'm too fat.

○ I'm ugly, homely, or unattractive.

○ I'm not intelligent enough, not smart enough.

○ I'm stupid.

○ I'm not creative enough.

○ I'm too selfish.

○ I'm too intense.

○ I'm too much, but I'm not sure what I'm too much of.

○ I'm too different.

○ I'm weird.

○ I'm scattered.

○ I make mistakes.

○ I have physical defects or imperfections.

○ I have problems.

○ I cry too easily.

○ I'm too emotional.

○ I'm not perfect.

☐ I'm gay or bisexual.

☐ I'm black, Hispanic, Asian, Indian, or Jewish, or belong to some other minority.

☐ I'm a loner.

☐ I don't have a partner.

☐ I'm afraid to be alone.

☐ I have fears.

☐ I have phobias.

☐ I'm not very talkative.

☐ I don't think quickly enough.

- ☐ I'm just like my father.
- ☐ I'm just like my mother.
- ☐ I can't take care of myself.
- ☐ I need a man to take care of me.
- ☐ I need a woman to take care of me.
- ☐ I can't make decisions.
- ☐ I'll never amount to anything.
- ☐ I can't tell jokes well.
- ☐ I'm too sensitive.
- ☐ I'm too insensitive.
- ☐ I'm too serious.
- ☐ I'm not serious enough.
- ☐ I think differently from other people.

False Beliefs about Control

- ☐ I can control how others feel and behave.
- ☐ I can control others liking or loving me, caring about me, respecting me, doing what I want.
- ☐ I can have control over whether people reject me.
- ☐ I can have control over someone desiring me sexually.
- ☐ I can have control over how others feel and behave by:
  - ○ Suffering, playing the martyr.
  - ○ Being right about everything.
  - ○ Scowling.
  - ○ Hitting, spanking.
  - ○ Changing the subject.
  - ○ Using sarcasm.

○ Raising my eyebrows.

○ Whining.

○ Shrugging my shoulders.

○ Making comparisons.

○ Throwing things.

○ Interrupting.

○ Telling my feelings.

○ Silent angry withdrawal.

○ Acting like a know-it-all.

○ Interpreting.

○ Pushing others into therapy.

○ The silent treatment.

○ Disapproving looks.

○ Disapproving sighs.

○ Exaggerating, catastrophizing.

○ Yelling.

○ Getting angry.

○ Criticizing, judging, shaming.

○ Saying "Tsk, tsk" and shaking my head.

○ Getting annoyed, irritated, short, curt.

○ Accusing.

○ Blaming.

○ Pouting, sulking.

○ Becoming ill.

○ Being sneaky or deceptive.

○ Lying or withholding the truth.

○ Therapizing, analyzing.

- Moralizing.
- Nagging.
- Lecturing, giving advice.
- Arguing.
- Explaining, convincing, selling.
- Becoming self-righteous.
- Talking incessantly.
- "Poor me" tears, blaming tears.
- Temper tantrums.
- Put-downs.
- A superior attitude.
- Half-truths.
- Being a "nice guy."
- Being financially successful.
- Achieving, being perfect.
- Giving gifts with strings attached.
- Being emotionally or financially indispensable.
- Complaining.
- Justifying.
- Interrogating.
- Denying.
- Talking others out of their feelings by telling them they are wrong.
- Asking leading questions, to which only one answer is acceptable.
- Bribery.
- Teaching, pointing things out without being asked.

○ Flattery or giving false compliments.

○ Giving in, giving myself up, going along.

○ Not asking for what I want, putting aside what I want.

○ Agreeing with others' points of view.

○ People pleasing.

○ Pulling energetically for attention or approval.

○ Rescuing.

○ Censoring what I say about what I want and feel.

○ Second-guessing and anticipating what others want.

○ Putting myself down.

○ Using threats of:

- Financial withdrawal.
- Emotional withdrawal.
- Sexual withdrawal.
- Exposure to others.
- Abandonment or leaving.
- Illness.
- Violence.
- Suicide.
- Alcohol or drug abuse.

False Beliefs about Resistance

☐ Resisting control is essential to my integrity and individuality.

☐ Resisting control establishes my independent identity.

☐ When another person is attempting to control me, my only choices are to comply or resist.

☐ I am really being my own person when I resist.

☐ It's the controlling person's fault that I resist.

☐ I can avoid being controlled by resisting.

☐ If I didn't resist, I would be swallowed up.

☐ I resist others' control by:

- ○ Doing nothing.

- ○ Saying I'll do what the other wants and then not doing it.

- ○ Doing the opposite of what they want.

- ○ Explaining, defending, or getting mad about why I shouldn't do it.

- ○ Getting critical and making them wrong for asking.

- ○ Saying I'll do it and then doing something else.

- ○ Saying I'll do it and then forgetting or failing to show up.

- ○ Procrastinating.

- ○ Acting helpless or incompetent.

- ○ Getting apathetic, having no enthusiasm.

- ○ Getting sick.

- ○ Being late.

- ○ Misunderstanding.

- ○ Doing what they want, but doing it halfway—doing a poor job.

- ○ Doing it wrong on purpose.

- ○ Finding some way to sabotage the situation.

- ○ Pretending not to hear.

- ○ Being uninterested.

○ Being closed to learning.

○ Refusing to make a commitment.

☐ Sometimes I resist other's control by shutting them out. I shut people out with:

○ Work.

○ Drugs or alcohol.

○ Hobbies.

○ Illness.

○ Meditation.

○ Reporting or storytelling.

○ Worrying.

○ Reading.

○ Sports.

○ Friends.

○ Spending money.

○ Watching TV.

○ Occupying myself with children.

○ Eating.

○ Depression.

○ Sleep.

○ Fantasizing or daydreaming.

○ Silent, angry withdrawal.

○ Headphones.

False Beliefs about God

☐ I have been abandoned by God because I am unworthy, bad, flawed, unlovable, or unimportant.

☐ God doesn't exist. I am ultimately alone, so I have to maintain control. There is nothing spiritual to turn to.

☐ If there is a God, then he/she/it would have done something about bad things happening. Therefore, God either doesn't exist or doesn't care.

☐ God is judgmental.

☐ God is too busy for me.

☐ God is there for some special people, but not for me.

I'm going to do a visualization to help you tune into how you developed your wounded self. Even though we're going to be going into the past and looking at what happened, it's not about blaming anybody; it's just about awareness.

When you do a visualization, relax into it. Again, if you find yourself wandering off, just bring yourself back in. You can record yourself reading this session, or you can have someone read it to you, maybe accompanied by soothing music.

Take some deep breaths. Scan your body and notice if there's any tension anywhere. Breathing into the tension, breathing in relaxation, breathing out the tension. Breathe into any parts of your body that feel tense and breathe that tension out.

Let yourself go back to a time when you were young. Remember your house, your room, your family, or remember not having a family or a house, or living with foster parents, or in an orphanage, or even on the streets. Do you think your parents or caregivers liked you? Did they think you were a wonderful person? Or was there always something wrong with you? Did you often feel you were just not good enough? Did you believe that maybe you were a bad person?

If you lived with your parents, how did they treat each other? Were they open and respectful? Was one angry and the other compliant or resistant? Were they both angry? Did they ignore each other? Were they shaming or blaming of each other? Did they nag at each other? Was there violence in your home?

How did your parents or other caregivers treat themselves? Did they abuse substances—alcohol, drugs, or food? Did one always put themselves aside for the other? Did your mother or caregiver allow herself to be physically or sexually abused? Did your father allow himself to be physically abused? Did either of your parents or other caregivers allow themselves to be emotionally abused?

Were one or both always overworked? Did either of them ever play? Did either of them ask for what they wanted? Did you see them taking responsibility for their own happiness? Were they happy some or much of the time? Was their joy in your home?

How did your parents or caregivers deal with pain? Did they see it as weak to show pain? Did you ever see either of them crying? If they did, were they victims? Or did they take responsibility for their pain? Were they there for each other when one was in pain? Were they there for you when you were in pain? Was anyone ever there for your pain? Or did you get the message that they could not handle their own pain or yours? Did they shame you for your pain and your tears?

How did your parents or other caregivers treat you when they were feeling needy, lonely, angry, anxious, overwhelmed, or drunk? Did they yell at you? Did they beat you? Did they sexually abuse you? Did they neglect or ignore you, smother you, shame you, threaten you, blame you, or nag at you?

Remember a time when you did something your parents or caregivers didn't like. Maybe you broke a toy, broke something of theirs, or did poorly in school. Maybe you cried, talked back, hit another child, or got into some other kind of trouble. How did your parents or caregivers handle it? Were they angry, violent, disapproving, hard, silent, critical, judgmental, shaming, cold, nagging? Or were they loving, understanding, caring, open? How did you feel if they were unloving to you?

If you had siblings, did you get along with them? Did you have a sibling who was mean to you? Did your parents or caregivers protect you from being harmed by your sibling? Or did they ignore the situation?

Did your parents or caregivers trust your experience? Or did they disbelieve you? When were you the one who was mean, did your parents ignore that?

When you did something positive, you accomplished something, you got good grades, you were kind to someone, you had a talent, how did they respond to you? Were they interested and loving? Or did they just ignore you?

Did your parents or caregivers attend important school events, or were they just too busy or uninterested? Did you feel important or unimportant to them? Did you ever feel that you were a bother or a burden? Or did your parents give you everything and you feel entitled?

Now take some deep breaths. Allow yourself to become aware of how you treat your own inner child. How is your wounded self like either or both of your parents or other caregivers? Let your awareness go inward and see what you do when you're operating out of your wounded self, when you're feeling angry, hurt, scared, alone, or in grief.

How do you handle difficult or painful feelings? Do you eat, take medication, drink alcohol, or use drugs? Do you get angry and blame others for your feelings? Do you feel that you're entitled to have others take responsibility for you? Do you ignore your feelings until they make you sick? Do you engage in activities such as work, sex, or TV, hoping to block them out? Do you discount your feelings as silly or overreactive? Do you criticize yourself for having these feelings, telling yourself that there's something wrong with you or that you're just too sensitive?

Do you run away, ignoring your feelings? Do you shut down, withdraw, go numb, resisting your feelings? Do you try to plug into someone else, hoping to get them to caretake your feelings? Do you caretake others' difficult or painful feelings while ignoring your own?

Now allow yourself to feel that child within you, breathing in. How do you, as the inner child, feel when your wounded self is in charge, ignoring you, criticizing you, discounting you, shutting down, running away or blotting out your feelings? How do you feel when your wounded self is shaming or indulgent? Do you feel alone, empty, sad, anxious, unimportant, angry, depressed, numbed out, victimized, scared, or overwhelmed?

Move inside your body. Feel what it's like to be alone within your body, with no loving adult there to love and care for you.

Now breathe into your heart, moving into a loving adult state, opening to learning. See your wounded self and your inner child, compassionately embracing these aspects of yourself. Bring love to both the wounded self and the inner child.

When this feels complete, open your eyes, and come back into the present.

Here's an exercise you can do to connect with your inner child. You may want to hold a stuffed animal in order to come into closer contact with that part of yourself.

In the first part, you tell your parents or caregivers—particularly the ones that you had problems with—how they treated you. In the second part, which is harder, you're going to let your inner child tell you how you're treating yourself.

I'm going to demonstrate this process from the perspective of when I started doing Inner Bonding, because today I don't have the same issues that I had then.

Mom, I just remember you yelling, I just don't remember you being warm or nurturing. I don't remember you ever standing up for me. I don't remember you teaching me anything about life or anything. I just remember you being annoyed with me, angry with me, like I was just a big bother to you. I don't remember you holding me. In fact, I can remember not even wanting to be held by you, because it felt like you were just a black hole sucking the life out of me. You never wanted to know anything about my feelings. My feelings didn't count. Just yours did.

Dad, you were a pretty good dad for the first twelve years.

Then you got it into your head—you told me later that you read that in some Indian tribes, the fathers taught the daughters about sex, so you decided that was your right. Of course, it was extremely trauma-tizing to have my dad, who I thought really loved me, trying to have sex with me. I had to stay away from you. I told you about it in my early twenties. You told me about this Indian thing. But you never got it. When you were dying, and I came to you to be with you and to love you, almost your last words to me were, "Oh, sweetheart, I wish I could make love to you." I know where you are now that you know how painful that was for me.

Grandma, I wish you hadn't lived with us. You were just mean. You were just mean to me all the time, always criticizing. Always trying to control everything I did. Always seeing me as bad.

Mom, you didn't protect me from my father. You knew what was going on. Because I asked you about it later, and you said, "Oh, I thought I stopped him," but you didn't. You didn't protect me from my grand-mother, and you knew what she was doing, because she did it to you, and you didn't stop her.

OK. Now I'm going to be my inner child. I'm going to talk to the wounded self I was before I started to do Inner Bonding.

You don't even know I'm here. I don't exist for you. You're never with me. You don't know what I feel about anything. The minute I'm upset, you go and take care of somebody. Or you overeat, or you distract yourself with work. You don't know I'm here. I am all alone inside. Everybody else is more important than I am. Everybody's feelings count, but mine don't. You are never here for me, ever. I don't think you know I'm in here. I am the best part of you. When is it my turn? When do I get to count? I'm making you sick, and I'm going to make you sicker. If you don't start to pay attention to me, we're going to die. I can't live this way, so you'd better start paying attention to me.

That was a real conversation, only it was a lot louder, because at that time, my inner child was absolutely enraged at me. When she said, "When is it my turn?" the rage in me was so big that I had to listen.

It was life-changing for me, because I realized I was going to die if I kept failing to take care of myself. I made two life-changing decisions at that moment that I kept forever: I decided that I was willing to be hurt, and I decided that I was willing to lose everybody else, but I was no longer willing to lose myself, because I knew that if I lost myself, that was it: I was going to die, and I wasn't ready to die.

I knew at that moment that it was going to be a tough challenge, because I had been such a good caretaker. I was Mother Earth: I took care of everybody, my husband, my kids, my parents, my clients, everybody, until there was nothing left of me.

I knew that if I stopped doing these things, it was going to be tough, and it was. I lost my marriage. My parents disowned me. Two of my three children were furious with me, but I got *me* back. My life started to change greatly for the better.

If you haven't been taking care of yourself, I know it's really hard to start loving yourself. But life opens up, everything opens up when you start to see, love, and value yourself and stop trying to control how everybody feels about you. That's what I was doing: trying to control how everybody felt about me. Life changed a lot for the better. It didn't feel like that at the time, but as I look back, they were probably the best decisions that I ever made in my life.

If you grew up with authoritarian parents, the wounded self might be very authoritarian. If you grew up with permissive parents, where everything was OK and they didn't care, you might be very permissive and indulgent in your wounded self. Sometimes, if you grew up with very controlling parents, you may have created a lot of resistance (which may take the form of procrastination, for example). That's where resistance comes from. Resistance means, "OK, I'm not going to let you control me." Unfortunately, what happens is that we create a controlling part of ourselves that tells us what to do, then we go into resistance to it.

You want to be aware of what state you're in. Remember that we move into our wounded self when our intention is to control and avoid our feelings and protect against pain. That's what triggers us into all of this. It's the path of fear.

When our intention is to be loving to ourselves and others, and we want to start making this connection, we move into a state of love. That's the state we need to be in in order to take loving care of ourselves. The body feels completely different. When we're in a loving adult state, there's a feeling of expansiveness. When you really are in a connected state, everything looks brighter, and you feel love for everybody and everything. It's the most wonderful feeling. That's what happens when we're truly open to learning and in a loving adult state.

Of course, there are many things we want from others, such as approval, love, respect, nurturing, honesty, validation, acceptance, attention, connection, and a sense that we're special.

There's nothing wrong with any of these things. The problem comes in when we try to have control over getting them. We might, for example, indulge in caretaking, going against what we're really feeling, distorting the truth, being submissive, playing the victim, trying to be sexy, or pretending to be interested in the other person when we're not. How often do those tactics work? Not often.

Again, there's nothing wrong with wanting those things—respect, love, attention, validation—but with these strategies, we don't get them. Instead, why don't you give them to yourself? We actually have a much better chance of being loved and respected by others when we love and respect ourselves, because people often tend to treat us the way we treat ourselves.

I used to wonder why I was getting treated so badly. I did not understand that people were treating me the way I was treating myself. It was as if I were wearing a sign saying, "Kick me." If somebody is treating you badly, you might look at whether that's mirroring how you're treating yourself.

Why, then, do we so often fail to give ourselves the caring, attention, respect, and understanding that we want from others? You might think you don't know how. You know what it's like for somebody else to give you these positive things, but you might not know how to do it for yourself. It might never have been modeled for you. Or you may have been taught that it's somehow bad or selfish.

Let's define selfishness for a moment. You are being selfish when you expect somebody to give themselves up for you, and you don't care about the effect that your behavior has on others. But taking loving care of yourself, filling yourself up with love, taking responsibility for your feelings so that you're making yourself happy and peaceful and able to share love with somebody—how are those things selfish?

There's a huge difference between selfishness and self-responsibility. I grew up being told that taking care of myself was selfish. If I didn't do what my mother or my grandmother wanted me to do, I was told I was selfish.

Note also that I'm not talking about selflessness. I'm talking about being self-responsible. Let's say you really need a massage. Usually you put your child to bed, but you ask your husband if he'll do it tonight, because maybe it is loving to you to get a massage that you really need. But if your husband isn't willing, and your child depends on you, then getting a massage might not be the loving thing to do.

We have to ask, what's in my highest good? What's loving to me right now? What's loving to us is going to be loving to those around us. It's never loving to us to behave in a way that is truly unloving to those around us. That's not in the highest good of our soul.

There can be a religious element in neglecting to give yourself love. Mother Teresa was obviously very giving, but she was also extremely depressed. She went from therapist to therapist, trying to understand why she was so giving and yet she was so depressed. If you ever watch films of her, you'll see that she was completely self-abandoning. She took no care of herself. That's why she was depressed.

It's wonderful to want to give, but we've got to take care of ourselves and give from a full place, not from a depleted place. We want to give because it gives us joy to give, not to get approval or to get into heaven. Giving is a very joyous thing. When we are giving to ourselves and filling ourselves with love, it's one of the most joyful things in the world. But that's not true if we're giving from a depleted place, or from a place where we're trying to get somebody else's approval. That's not true giving; it's giving to get.

Now I don't think Mother Teresa was giving to get at all; I think she got great joy out of giving, but she was abandoning herself in the process. You could see it if you ever watched her: you could see that poor woman was exhausted. People kept asking and asking, and she just never said no.

Some people will say that they can't give themselves acceptance about things they think are unacceptable. But that too becomes a vicious circle. The wounded self says you're unworthy; you're not acceptable. In fact, that's the foundation of the wounded self—the idea that you're not worthy of love, and you're only going to be worthy if somebody else loves you and proves to you that you're worthy.

If a baby is born, is that baby unworthy of love? No. How do you know that? The baby is worthy of love just because it is. Even if it's got problems, it's still worthy of love. Whatever is happening with the baby, it's still worthy of love.

That's us inside. That's our soul. We are inherently worthy of love because we are sparks of God, because we exist, because we have a soul inside of us. We have the sacred privilege of being adults who can take care of our soul.

Nonetheless, we have a wounded part that has disconnected us from who we are. It says, "You're not worthy of love," but the wounded self is really saying is that *it's* not worthy. We were created by God, but we made our wounded self. We created it; God didn't. It's always defective, because it's not real in the sense that our soul is real, and it's based on false beliefs.

When the wounded self says, "I'm not worthy," it's really talking about itself, not about who we really are, because it doesn't know who we are. A loving adult would say, "Well, I know you believe that, but I have a divine spark in me, who is deeply worthy of love. I'm also going to love you, my wounded self, because you're coming from false beliefs. I'm not going to jump in and judge you," because the loving adult doesn't judge. The more you do that, the more worthy you feel.

If you have a child, and you're constantly telling the child that it isn't worthy, it's going to feel unworthy. If you value the child, you see the child, you mirror the child, and you help the child to see who he or she really is, the child feels worthy. Telling yourself you're unworthy is a way the wounded self tries to get you to not love yourself. Because if you love yourself, the wounded self believes that it will be out of a job.

The wounded self might also tell you that if you love yourself and treat yourself well, you're going to do bad things or you won't be a good person. The wounded self makes up all kinds of lies.

Don Miguel Ruiz, author of *The Four Agreements*, also wrote a book called *The Voice of Knowledge*. He makes a really good point in it: the wounded self comes off as a voice of knowledge, but it's actually complete and total ignorance; it knows nothing. It is merely programmed; it only lies; it has no access to truth. When you say, "I'm not worthy of love," that's coming from a voice of lies, from a dark place within us that has no access to the light of truth.

Remember, there are two voices: the voice of fear and lies and the voice of love and truth. The voice of love and truth says, "Of course, you're worthy. You're a spark of the Divine; how could you not be?" The voice of the wounded says, "You're not worthy of love." Which one are you going to listen to? The voice that knows nothing and has no access to truth? Or the voice of truth, the voice of love, the voice that knows what it means to be loving, knows who you are, and knows that you are inherently worthy? Which voice are you going to listen to?

We all had to create our wounded self for our survival—to try to create a sense of safety. But safety does not come from the wounded self. True safety comes from being connected to our guidance. As you do this over and over and you see that you really are guided, the wounded self eventually lets go. The energy of the wounded self diminishes as we heal false beliefs. It just says, "OK, you're doing a better job of keeping us safe than I am." In my case, it said, "OK, I'm exhausted anyway from trying to keep us safe." It just let go.

This is not to say that my wounded self is 100 percent gone. Some people—though I've never met them personally—say that they had an experience of enlightenment in which suddenly their ego, the wounded self, was completely gone. I think it'd be great to have that experience, but I never have. In my experience, through practicing Inner Bonding, that part has just gotten very small. Very, very diminished.

In relationships, these are often two sides of the wounded self: the taker and the caretaker. When you're a caretaker, you sacrifice. You try to fix. You ignore your own feelings. You martyr yourself. You're always thinking of the other. You try to rescue. You might use apologizing as a form of control. You do for others what they need to be doing for themselves. Helicopter parents do things for their children that the children need to be doing for themselves. They often render their children incapable.

Caretakers also give unasked-for advice, thinking they know the right way for other people. It's not wrong to give advice, but it is unloving to give advice that the other person didn't ask for. What happens when you give adolescents or adults unwanted advice, even in dangerous situations? The other person will most likely ignore it or go into resistance and do the exact opposite.

Like caretakers, takers can play the victim. They use people. They can be demanding. They might take up all the space with excessive talking. They often use anger and blame.

The caretaker is usually often cognizant of others' boundaries but has no personal boundaries. By contrast, the taker has personal boundaries, but often violates the other's boundaries.

Remember, taking and caretaking are two sides of a wounded, dysfunctional system. Many relationship systems fall into this dynamic, but it does not work to create a loving relationship. Of course, the way out is for each person to learn to take care of themselves, so that they're not operating out of this dynamic. When they are each loving to themselves, they can come together to share their love.

If you're in this dynamic in your relationships and wondering why you don't feel connected, that's why. But since you can't make the other person change, what you can do is learn to take loving care of yourself.

Very often with people I work with, if one person in the relationship starts to be loving to themselves, the whole system will change and become much more loving. (Not always: in my own case, when I stopped caretaking and started to take loving care of myself, my marriage got worse.) But often, the person on the other end might say, "Wow! I like what's happening! What are you doing?" and start to practice Inner Bonding as well. That's what creates a loving relationship.

Questioner: So when a feeling of anxiety or scariness arises, that's a signal to do Inner Bonding work?

Margaret: Yes.

Questioner: What do you do when, say, you're at work? I think a lot of childhood stuff comes up in those situations. Do you try to postpone it, telling your inner child, "We're going to deal with this later?"

Margaret: It depends on the situation. With practice, when you've done the process enough, you get really fast at it, so you can do it right in the moment. If somebody is acting in a way that I find upsetting, I'll go right in and see if there's something I'm telling myself. I'll ask my guidance, "What do I need to do? How do I take care of myself?" and it can happen very fast. Sometimes I might excuse myself and go to the restroom to do a process. Sometimes I might need to say to my inner child, "I'm going to write a note, and we'll deal with this later."

It's important to practice bringing Inner Bonding into your life. You want to practice being in step 1—moving from your head into your body—all the time. That's having your inner baby monitor on: you want to be present in your body all the time. Step 1 takes a lot of practice, but you want to practice it until it becomes a natural way of being, so that you know the moment there's anything other than peace inside. Then you can go through the whole six steps. I'm doing it all the time. I'm not doing the six steps all the time, but I am doing step 1 all the time.

Jodi: When I first started working on this process a couple of years ago, someone who trained with you gave me an idea that helped me. I have a couple of reminders on my phone that pop up. One in the morning says, "How is little Jodi feeling?" Then I have one late in the afternoon that says, "I love you, and I'm listening." That helps to make sure that I'm checking in with myself twice a day and keep doing it.

Margaret: That's great. When I first started doing the process, I used a little thing called a MotivAtor, which you can buy online and set it to buzz against your body. I set it to buzz every five minutes, and then every ten minutes and then every half an hour, so I could remember.

A woman in one of my courses came up with a great idea. She found a picture of her inner child that she loves, and she put it on her phone. Every time she turns on her phone, she sees the picture. It reminds her to check in, because people use their phones all the time.

5

Who You Really Are

When you're operating as a loving adult and you're taking loving care of yourself, the core self gets to be who you really are. Here are some of its characteristics. The soul is:

- Joyful
- Kind
- Loving
- Empowered
- Good
- In the moment
- Worthy
- Brave
- Curious
- Playful
- Energetic
- Enthusiastic
- Grateful
- Positive, with up energy
- Thankful
- Empathic
- Creative

Look at this list. Is there anything that makes this soul, which is in all of us, unworthy of love?

When you're telling yourself you're unworthy of love, when you're in your wounded self, you're lying, because there is nothing here that is unworthy of love. This is who we are in our soul.

In addition, we also have special gifts. Somebody might be musically or artistically gifted, might have a particular kind of insight, or might be particularly empathic or clairvoyant. We all have special gifts, and we came here to express them. I believe that we're on the planet to evolve in our ability to love and express the gifts that we've been given. When we're operating from our wounded self, it's not going to happen. When we operate from our loving adult, and we value who we are inside, we evolve in our ability to love, and we allow ourselves to express the gifts that we've been given. It's very joyful to do that.

The soul is really big. I highly recommend Dr. Jill Bolte Taylor's book *My Stroke of Insight*. She is a brain scientist. When she was thirty-seven, she had a huge stroke in the left side of her brain. Her left brain went completely offline. When this happens, you forget your name, you forget phone numbers, you forget who people are. Being a brain scientist, she knew she was having a stroke. Fortunately, she got to the hospital.

Taylor was a scientist; she was not a spiritual person or even a particularly kind or loving person. When her left brain was offline, her right brain took over, and she was able to leave her body at will.

In her book, Taylor says she was shocked at how huge the soul is: it's way too big to fit into the body. Only a part of our soul comes into the body, and that's what we're calling the inner child. The rest of our soul is all around, and that's our higher self, our connection to Spirit.

We have two sources of guidance: our higher self and the soul within, which often communicates through feelings or intuition. We need these feelings; we don't want to be numbing them out or ignoring them. They have important information for us. Our inner guidance system lets us know instantly whether we're loving ourselves or abandoning ourselves.

That's important information to know, because if you're loving yourself, you're going to be feeling peaceful and happy. When you're abandoning yourself, you're going to feel wounded feelings, such as anxiety, depression, guilt, shame, anger, aloneness, emptiness, jealousy. They're letting you know that you're abandoning yourself: You're staying in your head, ignoring your feelings. You're judging yourself in some way. You're numbing yourself with addictions. You're making somebody else responsible. You're acting from your projections to avoid pain.

We need all our feelings. It's sad that in our society you're not supposed to feel anxious or depressed; we're told that you'd better do something to get rid of those feelings rather than looking at what you're doing to cause them, both physically and emotionally.

I'm going to do a visualization to help you connect with your higher guidance. To begin with, think about which figure or image would feel safe and comfortable for you. It may be Jesus, maybe God or the Buddha. It may be a personal guide. It may be a master teacher. It may be an inner mentor. It may be a guru, an angel. It may be just a light or your own higher self—an older, wiser part of you that you can turn to. It may be something you see or something you feel. It really doesn't matter; it's what works for you, because the information that you need is there. Visualizing helps some people. Others don't need to do that. All you need to know is that guidance is there.

I've never conceptualized God as a person. To me, God is love, God is peace, God is joy, God is wisdom. God is Spirit, the overall spirit of love and creation. God is the law of love. If you think about the law of gravity, for example, it applies to everybody equally. It doesn't matter whether you're acting lovingly or unlovingly: gravity is going to keep you on the ground; it's not going to say, "You've been bad today; I'm going to let you fly off the planet."

The love of God is also like the air we breathe: no matter who you are, if you take a breath, air is going to come into your lungs. The love that is God is like that; it is here. It is always here, but, like the breath, it can only come in by invitation. If you don't take a breath, the air cannot come into your lungs. God comes in by invitation. The invitation is your intention to learn about loving yourself.

When you say, "I want to learn about what's loving to me," you are inviting that presence. You can call it God or Spirit or Holy Spirit, or whatever you want. That presence is going to be there, but only by invitation. It cannot come in on its own, because we have free will.

When we're in our wounded self, there is no invitation. The wounded self is the part of us that believes in separation; it does not believe in oneness, and it thinks it knows better than God. Which tells you it doesn't know anything.

To do this exercise, first, you need to be willing to use your imagination. Our imagination is a gift.

It's a bridge that brings us into Spirit. When I was a kid and used my imagination, it was put down: "Oh, it's only your imagination." As if there's something wrong with that. There is not. Your imagination is a true gift.

Again, to do this practice, you can record yourself reading it, or you can have someone read it to you, perhaps with gentle music playing. One option is Metamusic: music created at the Monroe Institute in Virginia that has tones built in that help you to connect with Spirit.

Begin by breathing into any places that are tense. Breathe out the tension, breathe in the relaxation, and breathe out the tension. Imagine yourself in a beautiful place in nature, such as the ocean, a forest, a desert, or a meadow. Maybe there's a waterfall or a brook.

Imagine that you can feel the temperature of the air on your skin and hear the sounds of the birds or the water or the wind. You can smell the flowers, the trees, the salt of the air; you can even taste the air. Use all your senses as you imagine your beautiful place in nature. Imagine that you become aware of a warm, loving, powerful presence beside you. This presence is your spiritual guidance. Your guidance wants to come in whatever form feels comfortable for you.

You have an opportunity to imagine exactly how you want your guidance to appear to you. Depending on your worldview, imagine a being or energy within and/or without who for you is the most loving, powerful, and wise being or energy you could ever imagine. It could be a pure light or pure energy. It could be your experience of nature. It could animal or human. It could be Jesus, Buddha, Allah, Mother Mary, or one of the other saints. It could be someone you've known and loved who has died. It could be the highest, most glorious part of you, an older, wiser part of yourself. Or it could be an inner mentor, a spirit guide, a guardian angel, a teacher.

This presence could be something you see, or just something you feel: an energy of love and compassion, softness, gentleness, power, strength, and wisdom. Use your imagination and make up whatever feels totally safe, loving, wise, and powerful—the being or energy or light you would love to be held by or to feel within you. A being or energy or light you can turn to for love and guidance and wisdom and comfort whenever you want.

Imagine whatever feels most comfortable and safe for you. Imagine that this guidance is here now with you. Feel yourself surrounded by love and filled with love. Imagine that you can relax and rest in the love of your guidance, just letting go.

If this is a being other than your own higher self, or other than someone you know, you can make up a name for this being—whatever name you like. Or you just could call it "my guidance" or "my angel."

Imagine the peace that surrounds you and is within you as you are with this energy of love. Imagine that your guidance knows everything about you and loves you unconditionally. Imagine that your guidance never leaves you, is always with you and within you. This is your personal guidance, and you can always turn to it for love, wisdom, strength, and truth.

While you're in this beautiful place with your guidance, allow yourself to go back to a painful time in childhood—a time when you felt sad and lonely, maybe when you felt rejected at school or at home. Or when you had been abused physically, emotionally, or sexually. Or when you were left alone and neglected. Or when you feel shamed and hurt. Maybe when you were hospitalized and alone, maybe even as an infant alone in your crib, crying with no one coming.

Imagine yourself as that infant or child, alone in your room or in a crib, on the playground, in the hospital, or outside, lonely and in pain. See if you can feel that time when you felt so alone and afraid.

Imagine yourself as you are now, an adult coming into the place where you are as an infant or child, along with your higher guidance. Introduce yourself to yourself as a child, and imagine the wonder in your child's face as he or she recognizes you. Now take your inner child on your lap and proceed to become the most loving adult that you can imagine—holding, stroking, talking, reassuring, compassionately hearing the pain. If it's a memory of you as a baby, pick yourself up and rock yourself in a rocking chair, bringing divine love into yourself as a baby. Let your child know that you are now learning to love him or her so that you can always be here for him or her now that you're grown up. Imagine that you can feel your child relaxing against you with relief that you are here, right now.

Now imagine that you're with your child back in the beautiful place in nature that you imagined. Imagine you're sitting and holding your inner child, smelling the air, hearing the sounds, feeling the temperature on your skin, tasting the air.

Imagine that your guidance is with you, surrounding you and within you, while you're holding your child. Imagine that you can see your soul, your child, your essence, through the eyes of your higher guidance, through the eyes of love.

Look into your child's eyes and see who you really are. See your light, your goodness, your innocence, your vulnerability, your aliveness, your lovingness. See your child's joy and the special way your child laughs when he or she is happy. See your child's uniqueness, the special gifts that you've been given. See how very precious your inner child, your soul, is, how inherently lovable you are. See that your inner child as worthy of being loved and cared for by you. See that this little child just wants to be loved and be loving. See all the different ways he or she behaves when unloved or feeling afraid of being unloved.

Now imagine that surrounding your essence, your core self, your inner child, is your wounded self. Imagine seeing your wounded self through the eyes of your guidance. You can see the fear and the programmed beliefs and all the ways your wounded self tries to control out of fear. Feel the deep love and compassion of your guidance for your wounded self. Within your wounded self is your essence, your core self.

Notice that your wounded self doesn't even know anything about the beautiful light that is within. It is your responsibility to love both your wounded self and your core self, with the help of your guidance, in order to know who you really are.

Now pull your child into you. Pull in all his or her feelings, aliveness, passion, knowingness, sweetness, goodness, vulnerability, pain, fear, anger, joy. Feel your child within you.

You might want to imagine adopting your inner child, agreeing to take responsibility for defining your own worth and taking loving care of your own feeling. When you feel your child fully owned and within you, open your eyes and come back into the present.

Does anyone have questions about this practice or anything you'd like to share about this?

Questioner: It's hard to stay focused on it for me.

Margaret: Well, your wounded self doesn't want you to. The last thing in the world your wounded self wants is for you to connect with your guidance. Because when you really understand how powerful that is, you're going to stop listening to the voice of your wounded self.

Questioner: I was in a garden and asked for my guidance to appear. It appeared as a shiny, shimmering, rotating top.

Margaret: Yes, that's fine. It doesn't matter what form your guidance shows up in. It's just important that you start to interact, ask for truth, and ask for love and for loving action. Over time, you're going to understand that you really are being guided. We were not dropped on this planet alone; our guidance is always here for us, always loves us and always has our highest good at heart.

Questioner: If we have all this guidance, why do bad things happen to people? Like all the shootings that have happened recently?

Margaret: Yes, but that's the wounded self; that's what the wounded self does.

Questioner: No, no. I mean the people who were shot. Where was their guidance?

Margaret: Well, they might not have been open to it. With 9/11, there were people who said, "It's not a good day for me to go to work."

Most people are not taught to listen. I once had an experience when my kids were in high school in Los Angeles. A plane crashed that was going from Los Angeles to San Diego. Unfortunately, some of the parents from my kids' school were on it. One man had a friend taking him to the gate (at that time people could come with you to the gate) who could see people's auras. He said, "Don't get on this plane; everybody's aura is black." The man did not get on the plane. He didn't know how to see auras, but his friend did.

When I heard that, I decided I had to learn how to see auras. It's the kind of vision whereby you learn to look at a person, but you don't look at them; you sort of look past them. Unlike Erika, I can't see the colors, but I can see whether they're light or dark. I learned to do that after that incident, because it seemed like a good skill to know.

You've got to shift your vision; it's a particular kind of vision. Sometimes when I'm at a plane and I'm looking, I can see a person whose aura is darker; then I know they're probably ill, but if everybody's auras were dark, I wouldn't get on the plane.

Unfortunately, many people are told not to trust their inner knowing. They're not tuning in to where they should be or where they shouldn't be. On the other hand, as you'll see if you read Larry Dossey's book *One Mind*, many people do listen. They save their own lives; they save other people's lives; they know when something is happening to a grown child of theirs. It happens all the time. It's really a matter of developing awareness, and it's part of what happens when you practice Inner Bonding.

Let me go on to describe some of the things the loving adult does for the inner child:

- Nurture
- Listen
- Comfort
- Validate
- Be present
- Believe
- Love
- Encourage
- Trust
- Support
- Connect

Notice that these are the same things a loving parent would do with an actual child. That is exactly what we need to do with ourselves. That's what the loving adult does.

Loving adults also tune in. I had no brothers and sisters, so when I had kids, I did not know how to be a mom. When my son was crying, and I didn't know what to do, I would tune in: "OK: what does he need?" He couldn't tell me what he needed. I would think, "What does he need?" I would get information. When you want to be a loving parent, you naturally do that. You ask a question, and ideas will pop into your mind.

It's the same thing with ourselves. When you ask, "What would be loving to my inner child?" ideas will start to pop into your mind from your higher guidance.

Loving adults mirror our essence, as good parents mirror their children: "I loved how kind you were to your friend," or "Wow! That creativity amazes me." We need to do that kind of mirroring for ourselves, because most of us did not get it as we were growing up.

When I started to do this process, I did a painting that I really loved. Right away my wounded self came in and said, "Oh, it's just a fluke; you'll never do that again." I realized that that was a terrible thing to say to myself. At that moment I decided, "I'm not going to let those comments discourage me." I said to my inner child, "No, this is you. This is your creativity. Of course you can do it again!"

Then I started saying those things out loud any time I was kind, caring, insightful, or creative. I still do it. I thank my inner child all the time. "Thank you for your kindness. Thank you for your caring. Thank you for your empathy. Thank you for your creativity." That is very helpful in continuing to own who you are on the inner level.

When you're in your loving adult state, you hear information about yourself as a gift, because you want to learn. When you're in your wounded self, you hear the same information as an attack. If you're taking this information in this book as an attack, you are in your wounded self, but it's likely that you're reading this to learn something, so you're probably taking it as a gift.

When we're in the loving adult state, we are present, and we're not invested in the outcome. The wounded self is always invested in the outcome: "I'll do this so that will happen." The loving adult doesn't try and control outcomes; it's just present for what's happening.

Most of us did not get adequate mothering and fathering. We need to become the mother and father for ourselves. The mothering aspect—nurturing—is not enough in itself. We need to both nurture ourselves and take action for ourselves in the world.

Fathering is taking loving action. Loving fathering mean speaking up for us, standing up for ourselves. Step 5 is taking loving action, and that's the fathering aspect. The mothering aspect is the more internal aspect; the fathering is the more external.

When we're in the state of being loving adults, people can feel the difference in the energy. If you hug somebody when you're in your wounded self and therefore in a needy state, that person is going to feel a pull from you and will feel drained by your energy. If you're in a loving adult state, coming from a full place, and you're giving love, that person is going to feel energized by your hug.

Be very aware when you touch or hug somebody. Are you trying to get something? Or are you offering them love and positive energy?

I'd like you to do a little exercise now. I'd like you to take out a sheet of paper and write out a sentence, asking your inner child what your child wants from you as a loving adult: "What do you want from me as a loving adult?" You can use your nondominant hand if you want to; sometimes that make it easier to access the inner child.

When I started doing Inner Bonding and I asked that question, my inner child said, "I want you to see me and hear me. I want you to be present for me and speak up for me and take action for me. I want you to take care of me when I'm hurting and be caring and compassionate. I want you to listen to what's fun for me and take time to play and learn and grow."

Go ahead: ask your inner child. What does your child want from you as a loving adult?

Then, imagine your higher guidance, and ask your guidance, "What do you want to tell me about being a loving adult?" Write down whatever pops into your mind. Thoughts from the wounded self come *from* the mind, while thoughts from your higher guidance come *through* your mind, popping into your mind.

Questioner: What do you do when you can't remember a large part of your childhood?

Margaret: A lot of people can't, because it was painful. As you become a loving and trustworthy adult that your inner child can rely on to lovingly manage the pain, your inner child will let you in on the memories.

Questioner: What if you don't want to?

Margaret: Well, that's a problem, because your little girl needs you to know what happened to you. She's not going to tell you if you don't want her to, but as you develop your loving adult, you will want to know what happened. You will want to know where you got your beliefs, because the past can be healed. It's actually a big relief when people learn about their past, because it makes things make sense.

The child is not going to tell you until she trusts that you want to know, that you're going to care, and that you're going to be compassionate, believe her, and do the necessary work to heal the false beliefs. It's not so much the memories themselves, but the beliefs we formed around what happened that cause problems now.

A lot of people think that if they remember, they have to relive the pain. You don't. In fact, it's retraumatizing to relive pain. I work with people who have had extreme trauma. One technique I've used is called *revivification*: you see the memories on a screen, so you've got some separation from them; you don't have to feel them. You just have to see what happened and what you concluded as a result of it. Once you get that, you can let the memories go into the background. You don't need to keep on dealing with them.

Questioner: So for now, we would just go to the memory of what's wrong and deal with it from there, not needing to know where exactly the inner child is upset?

Margaret: No. Most of what you feel now is present. When you're going into feelings, you want to know what you're doing now, how you're treating yourself now. When we go down to the belief, that might open you up to the past. People assume that their pain is past when most of it is not. Most of it is current and has to do with how we treat ourselves.

Questioner: OK, yes, I was confused by that. I thought it was automatically my past.

Margaret: No, it's not at all. If you're treating yourself the way you were treated in the past, then you keep on retraumatizing yourself. You want to be looking at what's going on now; then the past opens up, and you see where you got the beliefs and the role modeling. That doesn't mean that you have to relive any pain. You don't. That is an old concept in psychology. It's a dangerous one, because it just keeps retraumatizing people.

Questioner: That's where the resistance is.

Margaret: Yes, that's right.

Questioner: Is there an easier way to remember the six steps?

Margaret: They're actually very logical. Think about what you would do with a child. The child's crying. What do you do? You go over; you want to know what's wrong. We're doing the same thing on the inner level. As I've said, many parents, without even thinking about it, will say, "How do I help my child?" They're getting ideas from Spirit, and they're taking some action and seeing if that helps the child. We're doing the same thing on the inner level. It's just that we don't think about doing that for ourselves the way we would for an actual child.

Questioner: Often people say, "The past is the past. You need to let it go. That story is over and done with." I'm a little confused, because if I am checking in with my wounded inner child and trying to revisit things that were done in the past, then I feel like I am going to perpetually be a victim. I am not letting that go.

Margaret: We don't let go of the past because we are continuing to treat ourselves in the way that we were treated in the past. We're operating from belief systems that we absorbed in the past, so saying, "The past is the past" doesn't really apply.

To really put the past in the past is to do what I've been talking about: you go deeper into "Where did I get these beliefs?" "Are they really true?" "What is true now?" "How am I treating myself based on what I absorbed in the past?" When you start loving yourself, the past really does go into the past.

Questioner: So will we ever truly be fully integrated?

Margaret: Well, it's just a process. People have this concept of getting there. But where is *there*? We're *there* any time we're in a truly connected state. We're there, but we don't stay there. Most people don't stay there because they're triggered by different things that happen. The more you practice Inner Bonding, the more moments you have of being there. It's just a process.

Heather: I struggle with procrastination.

Margaret: What's an area in which you procrastinate?

Heather: Oh, I procrastinate about everything, even pleasurable things.

Margaret: OK. Bring one up that you want to deal with.

Heather: I really want to deal with getting rid of the clutter in my house.

Margaret: OK. I want you to imagine that you decide you want to get rid of the clutter. OK? See if you can tune into what you feel as soon as you make that decision. What's going on inside of you?

Heather: I feel overwhelmed.

Margaret: OK, so breathe into the overwhelm. Get present with the overwhelm. Do you want responsibility for that overwhelm?

Heather: OK.

Margaret: Now breathe into your heart, and open to learning. Invite in the presence of love and compassion. Ask your little girl what you're telling her that makes her feel overwhelmed when you think about cleaning up the clutter. Then go inside to the part of you that feels overwhelmed. What does she want to say to you?

Heather: If I get rid of things, I'm going to regret it.

Margaret: OK.

Heather: Also that it's a waste.

Margaret: It's a waste, OK. Tune into how old were you when you got that concept, "If I get rid of things, I'll regret it, and it's a waste." How old do you think you were?

Heather: I have no idea.

Margaret: When did you start cluttering?

Heather: I've always been a collector as long as I can remember, since I was four or five years old.

Margaret: OK, so there's a young part of you that said, "It's a waste, and I'm going to regret it." Right?

Heather: Mm-hmm.

Margaret: Where do you think you got that idea at four or five?

Heather: I probably threw out something and regretted it, or it got thrown away, and I regretted it.

Margaret: You might have had a situation where you wish you hadn't had thrown something out, and you developed this belief that says, "If I throw it out, I'm going to regret it."

Heather: It still seems today that every time I get rid of something, a month or two later I need it, and I've got to buy another one.

Margaret: So having to buy the same thing again feels worse to you than having the clutter.

Heather: Yes. I feel, "You shouldn't have gotten rid of it."

Margaret: So you've said, "It's really important to me to get rid of the clutter," but there's something more important: not to throw out something that you're going to need at some point.

Heather: When I think about clutter right now, I'm thinking of going through all of my ridiculous amounts of jewelry and thinking, "It's crazy that I bought all that stuff."

Margaret: OK, but if you think about decluttering your jewelry, what do you feel?

Heather: I feel that it was wasteful, that I shouldn't have bought these things.

Margaret: A judgment comes in.

Heather: Yes.

Margaret: Then the wounded self comes in: "You shouldn't have bought it to begin with."

Heather: Right. I want to sell it. I want to try and sell things, but I never get around to doing it.

Margaret: OK, so when you think about selling, what are you telling yourself?

Heather: I don't want to have to deal with all the people that want to buy it.

Margaret: OK.

Heather: I just want someone to magically come and buy it.

Margaret: I want you to notice what's happening on the inner level here. There's one wounded part that says, "I should be selling my jewelry," and there's another wounded part that goes into resistance and says, "I don't want to have to deal with these people." Right?

Heather: Mm-hmm.

Margaret: Imagine a power struggle. Imagine that the wounded self that says, "I should be selling my jewelry," is one end of a rope. The one who says, "I don't want to deal with people who would buy it," is at the other end of a rope. Each one is tugging. That's called immobilization. Right? Nothing can happen as long as one part is saying, "This is what you should do," while another part is saying, "I don't want to do it." Right?

Heather: Right.

Margaret: Now I'd like you to breathe into your heart. Just breathe into your heart, and open to your higher guidance. Do you have a connection with your guidance?

Heather: Yes.

Margaret: OK. I want you to ask, "What is loving to me? What is in my highest good regarding the jewelry?"

Heather: To just get rid of it. Donate it. Just get rid of it. It's probably not going to be enough money to matter. It's not worth the aggravation.

Margaret: OK, so your higher guidance says, "Just clear it out. Just donate it. Just get rid of it." But there was also a wounded part that said what?

Heather: I feel like I'm being lazy by not selling it.

Margaret: OK, so that's another judgment: "I'm lazy."

Heather: I'm being lazy because I need to take pictures and put them online along with descriptions and measurements. How long are they? How wide are they? It's a hassle, but there the jewelry sits, taking up the entire bed of the guest room, and it's driving me bonkers.

Margaret: OK, but again, look at the dynamic. You go to your guidance. Maybe it's in your highest good to pack up and donate it, so you get a tax deduction. Immediately your wounded self comes in and says, "Oh, you're just lazy." Which voice are you going to listen to?

Heather: Unknown. I'm not sure. I should listen to—

Margaret: There is no *should*.

Heather: My highest guidance: it would be for my benefit.

Margaret: It just depends on your intention. The wounded voice is the voice of control, of fear, of lies. The voice of your guidance is the voice of love and truth, but your wounded self is coming in very quickly. You're listening to that voice, and that keeps you stuck. Now, if your intention is really to love yourself, what would you do?

Heather: I would get rid of the jewelry.

Margaret: That's right. You have to see that you have a choice here: you can either love yourself and get rid of it, or you can protect and avoid and control and listen to the voice of the wounded self: "Oh, you should be selling it. You should do this. You should do that." It's obvious that what's loving to yourself is to gather up what you don't want and donate it. Now imagine doing that. Imagine doing what your guidance says is in your highest good.

Heather: That's high anxiety.

Margaret: OK. Now tune into what you just told yourself that created the anxiety.

Heather: It's something I always say: maybe I could use them again.

Margaret: So it's the same "I'm going to get rid of something I want. Maybe I could use it again." Which voice do you want to listen to?

The anxiety is your inner child letting you know that you've put your wounded self in charge again. Imagine gathering up what you don't use and donating it, and asking your wounded self right now to step aside. Just be quiet for a moment, and say to her, "Honey, step back. You don't know what you're talking about. You're making us stuck, so just be quiet." Imagine donating the jewelry without that voice. What do you feel?

Heather: Relief.

Margaret: The relief lets you know that that is indeed what's in your highest good. Again, it comes down to your intention. Either your intention is to be loving to yourself and bring relief, or your intention is to control—"Uh-oh, I might give something away that I'm going to want"—and to allow the wounded self to take over. That creates procrastination. If your whole focus were on loving yourself, you would just be asking your guidance, and you would do it.

Heather: What about procrastinating about doing my work stuff? That's driving me crazy.

Margaret: What's the issue with the work stuff?

Heather: I am going back to work in June. I am a tour director, so I am on the microphone on the bus all day, talking about the history of the places I go to. I have to have all my handouts ready, but I have nothing prepared. I don't even know where my stuff is. I don't even know where I threw it in November. It's in some closet.

Margaret: OK. Tune into the part of you that's saying, "I have to get this done." How old is that part that is controlling and telling you what you have to do?

Heather: Seven.

Margaret: Seven. What was happening at seven?

Heather: I had to clean my room.

Margaret: Now we're getting down to when this started. Was it your mother that said you have to clean your room?

Heather: Yes.

Margaret: How did you respond to that?

Heather: Freaked out. Tantrum. Drama.

Margaret: You went into resistance: "I don't want to be controlled by you."

Heather: Yes.

Margaret: OK, so now you've got your mother's voice in you. An aspect of your wounded self, maybe an adolescent aspect, is saying, "You have to get busy and find all that. You have to get to work."

Heather: Right.

Margaret: Then you've got a seven-year-old that's saying, "You're not the boss of me. I don't have to do what you want. I'm going to have a tantrum," and it goes into resistance. Right?

Heather: Right.

Margaret: Again, imagine the rope. You've got one part of you saying, "You have to get the work done," and you have another part of you saying, "You can't make me." Right?

Heather: Uh-huh.

Margaret: As long as these two parts of your wounded self are in charge, you're stuck; you're immobilized. Now again, go to your guidance and say, "What is in my highest good? What is loving to me?"

Heather: To get everything prepared so I can relax.

Margaret: Now see if you can tune into what you want to do. Do you want to get everything prepared so you can relax?

Heather: I want to be prepared. I don't want to do it. I want it to miraculously happen.

Margaret: OK, but it's not going to.

Heather: Exactly. I know I have a lot of magical thinking.

Margaret: So which is more important, to be relaxed or to not be controlled by your wounded self?

Heather: It's more important to be relaxed, but I do well with last-minute panic.

Margaret: OK, but then it's not more important; don't kid yourself. If it were more important to be relaxed, you would go ahead and do it because you want to be relaxed, but it's not. It's more important to you to be in resistance to being controlled, so you have to be honest.

Heather: How do I stop that?

Margaret: It's up to you. It's just about what's your highest priority. See, we fool ourselves regarding our highest priority. You think your highest priority is to be relaxed. It's not. It's to avoid being controlled by the other part of your wounded self.

When you tell yourself, "You should do this; you have to do this," those words are death for some-body who learned resistance as a kid: "should," "have to." The only time that you're really going to get to it is when you find the place in you that wants to be relaxed by getting it done. It's a want, not a have to. We do what we want to do, but many people have learned to resist what they tell themselves they should do or have to do.

Heather: How do I get myself to want more to relax?

Margaret: See, that again is you trying to get yourself to—it's just what you want. It's just what's most important to you.

Heather: It's almost like a bad habit. I've been so habituated to the drama, it's like I'm addicted to the drama.

Margaret: What you want is to not be controlled by your mother who's in you. Your mother's voice is in you.

Heather: Right.

Margaret: Your highest priority is to not be con-trolled by her. You need to own that. As long as that's what's most important to you—your high-est priority—you're going to resist. When it's more important to you to be loving to yourself and take care of these details so that you can relax, you will find it very easy to do.

Heather: So I need to think of it as giving yourself the gift of getting prepared in advance so you can relax?

Margaret: Yes, because that's what you want. It's not a have to, because you can wait. You can panic. You can do it at the last minute. You can make resistance and not being controlled your highest priority. You have every right to do that.

Heather: Oh, my gosh.

Margaret: It is a choice.

Heather: It might be a game changer to think of it that way.

Margaret: It is, once you really tune into what you want.

Heather: I feel weird saying this, but here's another thing I'm procrastinating about. This is going to sound insane or pathological, but if I have to go to the bathroom, I will put it off and put it off. I just don't want to. It still feels like I'm being told to do something. It's crazy.

Margaret: You'd be surprised how many people have that issue with having to go to the bathroom.

Heather: Oh, my God. Thank you.

Margaret: Yes. This is not an unusual issue.

Heather: Really?

Margaret: Your body is telling you what you have to do, and your seven-year-old is saying, "You can't make me. You're not the boss of me. I don't have to."

Heather: That's the way I feel.

Margaret: I know.

Heather: I feel annoyed.

Margaret: But that's a seven-year-old. That's not a loving adult. Again, not being controlled in that situation is a higher priority than being loving to yourself. The underlying issue is what the priority is. Because your mother was controlling and because you hated being controlled, you dug in, and you're still digging in. For all these years, not being controlled has had a higher priority for you than being loving to yourself. Do you see that?

Heather: God, it's so simple when you say it.

Margaret: Yes, but it's very deep; it's a very deep issue to not want to be controlled. That's the difference between "I have to go to the bathroom" and "I want to, because I want to feel better."

Heather: Oh, my gosh. I feel kind of liberated.

Margaret: That's the relief that lets you know what's loving to you.

Heather: Ask me five minutes from now, but for the moment, I don't feel a battle inside me.

Margaret: Right. Any time you do, you need to realize that those two parts of you are in that power struggle. The intention is to control and not be controlled. One part wants control; the other one doesn't want to be controlled. There you are, stuck.

Heather: Excellent. Thank you.

Margaret: You're welcome. This problem occurs when parents are very controlling with their kids, because most of us hate to be controlled. We might give in in certain situations, but resist in others. It follows many people up into their adult lives. They don't realize that a power struggle is still going on, but now it's internal. It stops them from doing what they really want to do and what's really loving to themselves. Any questions about that?

Questioner: Yes. I'm assuming all of us have this issue with our parents and the "shoulds" and "you'd betters." What would it look like, what would a loving adult say to a child instead of, "You'd better clean up your room, young lady"? What does a loving adult say to encourage that child to clean the room without getting into this condition of controlling and resisting control?

Margaret: With my kids, there were a lot of areas that I just didn't enter into, like their schoolwork.

When they first started school, I said to them, "School is your responsibility, not mine. If you want to do well, you can do well. If you don't want to, that's fine. I will love you either way. It's not my job, but if you need my help, you can ask me." I didn't know when they had homework or they had tests unless they asked me for help. They were all self-motivated; they all did really well, because nobody was pushing them.

With things like brushing teeth, I had told them, and I would remind them one time each evening: "If you get cavities because you didn't brush your teeth, you have to pay for them out of your birthday money or holiday money. If you lose a jacket at school out of carelessness, you have to buy yourself a new one." They knew the consequences.

I never had any problems with bedtime, because they knew that at a certain time, let's say 8:00 p.m., I was available to spend time with each of them— good time, reading time, talking time, connected time. They could go to bed anytime they wanted, but if they wanted me there, they had to be ready at that time. They could do whatever they wanted, but they had to deal with the consequences of being tired. Each of my three kids tested it out one time. They were not happy with being tired. They did not like not having me there. That was the end of it. It's not trying to control them; it's deciding what's loving to you.

It was loving to tell my children the consequences—paying for their teeth or their jacket or not being available at any old time except bedtime. I taught them how to read a clock and how to set their alarm when they were very young. It was their responsibility to get up in time. If they didn't, they would have to go in the carpool in their pajamas. It happened to one child one time, and that was it. It never happened again.

Questioner: Yes, so from the parent's standpoint, the parent is no longer saying, "What are you doing to me? Look what you're doing to me."

Margaret: That's right.

Questioner: "You're not cleaning your room. You're killing me." It's not that.

Margaret: No. It's not. You're not taking it personally. You're just deciding what's loving to you and what the appropriate consequences would be, which is a very good way of teaching responsibility to children.

Questioner: So how can we apply that to our inner child work? Can I say to myself, "If you go for a walk today, you're going to feel so good. You have a choice, and if you don't go"—

Margaret: No. It's not the child who decides. You can check in and see what you feel like doing, but you're the adult. You get to decide.

Questioner: Yes, but I'm still resisting that "should."

Margaret: OK, but then you need to realize that if you've got a "should," you have put your wounded self in charge, not your loving adult. The loving adult never has a "should." It's always a "want to."

Questioner: So it's "Do I want to take a walk?"

Margaret: Yes.

Danielle: To feel great.

Margaret: Yes. Do I want to? I've been walking for fifty years, just about every day, up and down hills. I want to. There's no struggle. I love it, so I don't have to force myself into it. I love how I feel when I'm outside. I do my Inner Bonding work. I love it, so of course I'm going to do it. I'm going to do what I love.

Questioner: About the work that you just did: it seems like we could all go through that process, and it can take a while to identify. So what aspects can we look out for while we're navigating through the process? I gather that we need to watch out for judgment by our wounded self and watch out for conflicting reasoning.

Margaret: Yes, but all of that is about control. Judgment is about control. The bottom line is, there's a part of your wounded self that's trying to control you, and then there's a part that doesn't want to be controlled. That's what you want to look for. There are many ways of trying to control, and judgment is one of them, telling yourself: "You should do this. You've got to do that."

It all comes down to intention. That's why it's so important to become aware of your intention, because that governs everything else. If it were more important to Heather to keep from giving something away that she would regret, then she would be stuck, but if it was more important to her to feel the relief of clearing things out, she'd do it, because that's what's loving to her.

Questioner: I want to go back to the practice that you just did. Thank you for that, because I just noticed, oh, my gosh, that's me. I think I resist everything, especially at work. I've noticed that as soon as I get any "shoulds"—say, "I should do A, B, and C"—I quickly revert back to "I don't want to. Just because you said that I should do A, I'm going to do C, and I want to do C." I justify myself. It's programmed in me. As soon as someone says, "You should do this," my inner response is, "I shouldn't do that. I should be doing B and C, and I know why." I have a whole story. How to come out of that?

Margaret: It's basically the same thing. If somebody tells me what I should do, I go inside, breathe into my heart, go to my guidance, and ask, "This is what they tell me I should do. What's in my highest good?" I make it irrelevant to me whether somebody is trying to control me or not. I had very controlling parents, and I know what it's like to want to resist. That doesn't feel good to me at this point in my life, so I basically make it irrelevant if someone is trying to control me or is telling me what I "should" do.

If somebody wants to control me, that's their issue. I don't become reactive if somebody says, "You should do this," or "I want you to do this," or "You'd better do that." I go in and say, "Is it in my highest good to do it, or is it in my highest good not to do it?" If it's in my highest good to do it, I'll do it. If it's not loving to me to do it, then I say no. I decide with my guidance. I don't allow them to put me into a reactive position or define who I'm going to be at any given moment.

By going to my guidance and asking what's loving to me, I am free of the dynamic of control. I don't care if they think they've controlled me. I am free to do what's best for me. That takes me completely out of that control-resistance dynamic. Do you see what I mean?

Questioner: Yes. I'm just thinking how it might get tricky in a personal relationship versus a professional relationship.

Margaret: It's really the same thing. Whether it's personal or professional, I do the same thing. I go inside and ask if it's loving to me.

Questioner: I too struggle with procrastination. I had a very loving but highly critical and perfectionistic father. When I lived with him, he was a taskmaster. There was only one way to do things, and it was his way. If I was doing something about which he had given very specific instructions, as soon as I made an error, he would take the task away from me. He would complete it because I'd messed up. I have projects around the home that have sat for years half completed because I'm waiting on a man who is now dead to come home and finish them for me.

Margaret: So you've got his voice in you now.

Questioner: Saying, "You can't do it right." I started removing the wallpaper in my downstairs bathroom. It's half done, but as soon as I make an error, I stop. Now there's only half of the wallpaper.

Margaret: OK, but what would your loving adult do? If you're not operating out of your wounded self, it's fine to make mistakes. I say to my little girl, "I don't care how many mistakes you make. I don't care how often you fail. I'm going to love you anyway." That gives me freedom. That gives me the freedom to fall on my face, make a fool out of myself, and make mistakes. We all need that freedom. You didn't grow up with that freedom, but you can give it to yourself.

Questioner: Probably every room in my home has something that I have started—

Margaret: OK, but you can give yourself the freedom now by telling yourself, "It's OK to fail. It's OK to make mistakes. It's OK to not be perfect. I will love you anyway." Your little girl needs to know that she can go ahead and do these projects and mess up. You're not going to be your father. You're not going to be critical. You're not going to tell her she's done it badly or wrong. You're going to say, "It's OK. I love you anyway," and show that loving her does not depend on her doing this project well.

Questioner: It's OK.

Margaret: It's so important to give yourself the room to mess up, to make mistakes, to fail. One thing that has allowed me to take risks in my life— and I take many—is that it's 100 percent OK with me to fail and make mistakes. My little girl knows that I love her, not because of what she does, not because of her accomplishments, but because of who she is as a soul. This is important for your freedom to manifest what you want in your life and to complete what you want to complete. To be able to express yourself is to get yourself off the hook from having to do it right, from not being allowed to make mistakes. Only we can give this to ourselves. Nobody else can give it to us.

6

Step 1 in Detail

At this point, let's focus on step 1, which is the willingness to feel pain and fear and take responsibility for our feelings. Willingness means that you're willing to do whatever it takes to heal: there are no conditions under which you're not willing to do the work that you need to do. You're willing to take responsibility for your sense of safety, your sense of worth, your feeling lovable, for your joy, for your pain. You're willing to take emotional responsibility as well as physical, financial, organizational, spiritual, and relational responsibility. We need to function well in these six areas for our inner child to really feel well taken care of. The inner child feels worthy, loved, and valuable when you take responsibility in these areas, and feels unloved and unimportant when you don't.

Some people show up well in one or two of those areas. Maybe you take really good care of yourself financially, but you're not taking care of yourself emotionally or organizationally. When we talk about problems with clutter or not getting to work on time, that's a matter of not taking care of yourself on the level of organization. Being on time, keeping your environment workable—that's organizational responsibility.

Step 1 is, as you've seen, breathing in: using your breath to get inside your body—tuning in to what you feel on the physical level, because feelings generally show up physically. Anxiety, for example, will show up as tightness in your stomach or in your throat. Depression might be a heaviness in your heart. Feelings show up physically, so you want to be scanning your body on the physical level.

To really be responsible for your feelings, you have to be willing to face the deeper, core painful feelings that we all learned to avoid when we were little: the loneliness, the heartbreak, the grief, the helplessness over others, the sorrow over seeing people hurt each other. These are deep, core painful feelings. We need to be willing to feel them with compassion and learn how to be with them and let them move out of our being. If you avoid those feelings, you're going to be operating out of your wounded self.

Wounded feelings come from the thoughts and actions of the wounded self: thinking lies, telling yourself things that are not true, taking actions that are hurtful to you. These things cause our wounded feelings. The core pain comes from our environment, how people treat us, and what's happening in situations.

Start by tuning into your body; notice what these physical sensations are telling you. That's step 1: being present with your feelings so that you can learn what they're telling you. If you tune in, and you feel peaceful, excited, energized, joyful, and loving towards others, then you know you're taking really good care of yourself.

As I've said, these feelings are a source of inner guidance. You can't actually know what's right or wrong for you unless you're in touch with your feelings. How are you going to know what's right or wrong for you if you can't feel it? This is our intuition, our inner knowing. It lets us know what's right and good for us and what's wrong and bad for us. We need these feelings. We don't want to be numbing them out in any way.

There is a big difference between the feeling of aloneness and loneliness. Aloneness is what we feel when we've abandoned ourselves, and our inner child feels cut off and alone inside. Loneliness is a core feeling of life. That's when we want to connect with others, we want to share love, we want to have fun with someone and play with someone, but there's nobody around to connect with, or the person is not available. It's a very hard feeling, but it's very common. We need to be able to honor the feeling, have compassion for it, and then maybe take a loving action, such as finding people we can connect with, rather than being a victim of isolation or being with people who aren't going to connect with us.

Step 1 is about being willing to feel our pain, but we have many false beliefs that keep us from being willing to feel pain. What comes up for you when you think about being willing to feel pain? What are some of the false beliefs that you have about pain?

Questioner: That it's weakness.

Margaret: It's weakness. It's weak to feel pain.

Questioner: Rejection.

Margaret: I'm going to be rejected if I feel pain. What else?

Questioner: It has no end.

Margaret: There's no end. It's going to go on forever.

Questioner: Nobody wants to hear about it.

Margaret: Nobody wants to hear about my pain.

Questioner: It will make me crazy.

Margaret: I'll go crazy. I won't be able to function. Anything else?

Questioner: It doesn't fix anything.

Margaret: What's the point? Why cry over spilled milk? It doesn't fix anything. Most of us grew up with these beliefs. They may have been true for us as children. As children, the pain might have been unending. We needed to disconnect. We might have been rejected for our pain. But it's not true now when you learn to love yourself. Now being willing to feel your pain is a sign of strength, not a weakness. We can only do something about it is if we're open to the pain and seeing what we're doing to cause it or what's happening externally that's causing it. These beliefs stop people because they're locked into the false beliefs of the wounded self, but they're not accurate today.

There are two intentions regarding pain: There's open pain, which is when we're open to learning and we want to learn from our pain and we know that our pain has much to teach us. Then there's closed pain. That's the pain of the victim. That's "Poor me. Look what life is doing to me. Look what this person is doing to me. Look what

God is doing to me." That pain will go on forever. That's a stuck place, because there's no intention to learn about what you might be doing to cause it or what's happening with somebody else that you need to attend to.

Victim pain is a very stuck place. It's coming from the wounded self. When you're in it, you're totally closed up. You don't want any responsibility for your feelings. That's what causes suffering. Although there's pain in life, that doesn't mean we have to suffer.

The existential pain of life is loneliness, when we want to connect and nobody's there. Or heartbreak, when people have been mean and unloving. Grief: when people die, when there's loss. Helplessness over other people's behavior towards us, towards themselves, towards others.

One of the hardest pains of life is helplessness. Helplessness over others is hard partly because when you were an infant, if you cried and nobody came, that created a life-or-death situation for you. If the infant cries long enough and nobody comes in, it will die. The infant is not only helpless over others, but also over itself. When you're left to cry like that, you establish the belief that helplessness is life-threatening—which it was when you were an infant.

As adults, we are no longer helpless over ourselves. We are still helpless over others, but most people don't want to accept that, because it feels life-threatening. They'll do anything to try and control other people rather than say, "I'm helpless over this person. It feels awful, but that's the reality, and I'm going to embrace it with compassion."

With core pain, I suggest that first of all, you name it: "OK, honey, I know that you're feeling helpless over that person or situation, and you are. There's nothing we can do about the situation, but I'm right here. I'm with you. I'm not going to leave you. It's OK to feel this feeling. We're not going to die. I'll stay with you until you're ready to release it." We are not helpless with ourselves as we were as infants. We can take loving action for ourselves. It only takes a few minutes of this comforting before my inner child is ready to let it go. I say, "I give it to God. I ask for peace and acceptance to replace it."

When you attend to the pain, it really is not the big deal you think it's going to be, even though it was a huge deal when you were a child. When we were children, our bodies were too small to manage these big, painful feelings. We had to avoid them. For adults, it's manageable with love and compassion. Even with grief, even with losing someone you love. Grief comes in waves. Every time it comes, say, "Honey, I'm right here with you. I know you're so, so sad. This is such a huge loss. I'm right here with you. I'm not going to leave you alone." The grief will move through for that time, even if comes up again in five minutes. It's very important to learn how to lovingly manage these feelings.

Questioner: When I was in college, and even before that, I struggled with such acute depression and anxiety that I couldn't function. I had to drop out of school, and it was debilitating. At that time, I went on medication. Since then, I've made many attempts to go off the medication, but it's always been disastrous. I believe that I have a major depressive disorder, generalized anxiety, and all these other conditions. I've made it part of my identity. It's difficult now, because I've come to understand more about the trauma and how that has affected the depression and anxiety, but I've been stuck on these meds.

Margaret: What I want to suggest to you is not to worry about the meds right now. Practice Inner Bonding. Develop your loving adult. Start to take care of your little girl in the way she needs. Learn to stop retraumatizing yourself from your wounded self. Then you will reach a place where you don't want the drugs anymore. It won't be a disaster to go off of them, because you will have replaced them with loving yourself. Don't worry about it right now, and don't worry about how long it takes.

Just keep developing your loving adult, and there will come a point where you'll say, "I know I don't need these anymore. I'm going to be fine." I've worked with many people who have had severe anxiety and depression for years and years but were able to get off the meds when they learned to love themselves.

Ultimately, there is no process for getting into step 1, because it's just a matter of choice. Either you choose to be willing, to take responsibility for your feelings, or you choose not to.

Beliefs That May Be in the Way of Taking Responsibility for Yourself

Mark the beliefs that may be in the way of your willingness. Try to mark the beliefs that you feel in your wounded self. Your conscious mind might say, "I know this isn't true," but you may be operating from them nevertheless.

☐ I am not causing my feelings. My feelings are being caused by someone or something else, so there is no reason for me to explore them.

☐ I am right. Others need to change, not me.

☐ If I take responsibility for myself, I have to give up hoping that someone else will do it for me and believing that someone else taking care of me will make me happy and safe. I would rather keep hoping that someone will give me what I never got as I was growing up, and believing that this is the answer to healing my misery, even if I have to stay in pain.

☐ If I discover that I am responsible for my own feelings, I will feel like destroying myself.

☐ I am incapable of taking care of my own feelings. I'm afraid of failing at taking care of myself.

☐ If I look within, I will discover that my core is bad, wrong, or unworthy.

☐ If I look within, I will discover that there is nothing there.

☐ This process is too much work. It takes up too much energy. I don't have the time.

☐ I am in crisis now, so there is no time to take care of myself.

☐ Others are in crisis now, so there is no time to take care of myself.

☐ If I open, there will be too much anger for me to handle—at myself or at others.

☐ I cannot handle my pain, especially from rejection, abandonment, aloneness, and loneliness. I will explode, die, or go crazy if I feel my pain.

☐ If I open, I will be vulnerable to being controlled by my inner child, by others, or by God.

☐ My inner child is too demanding and needy.

☐ Resisting control by my own desires, or anyone else's, is more important than loving myself or others.

☐ If I open, I will lose control over the people and events that can cause my pain of aloneness and engulfment.

☐ It's not my job to make myself happy: others can and should make up for what I lacked as a child. The job belongs to my:

    ○ Parents.

    ○ Siblings or other family members.

    ○ Mate.

    ○ Boss.

    ○ Therapist.

    ○ Children.

    ○ Future mate.

    ○ Friends.

    ○ Minister, priest, rabbi.

☐ My best feelings come from outside myself, so there is no point in trying to make myself happy.

☐ Others' love and approval is what makes me happiest.

☐ Getting love from others feels better than giving it to myself and others.

☐ My lovability and worth come from others' attention, love, and approval, so there is no point in giving it to myself.

☐ I will have to confront an inner conflict between my core self and my wounded self about where I live, the work I do, the relationship I am in, or whether or not I want to have a family. I will have to make changes that will make me more unhappy than I am now.

☐ If I open to learning and growing, I will outgrow my relationship, and I will be more unhappy than I am now.

☐ If I take care of myself, I will end up alone.

☐ I have to be needy for someone to want to be with me.

☐ I would be too powerful, and no one would want me.

☐ I don't have the right to take care of myself.

☐ Taking care of myself is selfish.

☐ I don't deserve to be happy.

☐ If I take care of myself and make myself happy, others will:

- ○ Be angry at me.
- ○ Disapprove of me.
- ○ Withdraw and disconnect from me.
- ○ Withhold something from me.
- ○ Reject me.
- ○ Leave me.
- ○ Get violent with me or even kill me.
- ○ Judge me as stupid or as a failure.
- ○ Attempt to take advantage of me in some way.

And I will be more miserable than I am now.

☐ If others I love disconnect from me and take their love away, I cannot survive, so I have to give myself up to be loved by them.

☐ God/Higher Power has abandoned me or doesn't exist, so I have to stay in control. I am ultimately alone; there is nothing spiritual to turn to, nothing to open to and surrender to, no one to help me.

☐ I have to do everything myself. Therefore, I believe there is no point in opening: I will just feel more alone.

7

The Three-Step Anger Process

I want to talk about what it really means to be in an intention to learn. You have to believe that we always have very good and compelling reasons for our feelings and behavior. If you don't understand that our unloving behavior comes from our fears and false beliefs, you're going to be judging yourself; you can't learn. Learning doesn't happen when we judge ourselves.

We need to be compassionate for our woundedness, for the things we've done that have been hurtful to ourselves and others. Otherwise, we get stuck in judging ourselves, and that leads to getting even more stuck.

When you say to yourself, "I must have had a very good reason for doing what I did; I must have a very good reason for procrastinating; I must have a very good reason for being angry and losing it and going off the rails; I must have a very good reason for whatever I'm doing that's making me feel so anxious or so depressed," you open the door to learning and healing.

Saying that to yourself—"I must have a very good reason"—opens the door for exploration, which is what we want. We want to be able to explore our fears, our false beliefs, which are leading us to feel bad. This is also true with somebody else: that person must have a very good reason for behaving this way. This opens you to the intention to learn with a partner or a child or somebody that's important to you. We always have very good, compelling, important reasons for our fears and false beliefs. You're not going to move into compassion unless you remember that.

In step 2, we're saying, "OK. I am willing to take responsibility, and I'm going to move into this intention to learn." Again, you're not going to be attached to the outcome. If you're saying, "I'm going to do this so I can get rid of pain," or "I'm going to open to learning so then maybe I can find a partner," or "Then maybe I'll get approval"— these are all agendas. The point here is to love for the sake of love, without an agenda for what you're going to get. "I'm going to get money." "I'm going to get acclaim." "I'm going to get a partner"—that's all about control. The minute you're attached to the outcome, it's all about control.

In step 2, you're moving into your heart. You're breathing into your heart. You're making a conscious decision to open to learning, knowing you have very good reasons for whatever is going on. You're inviting in the love, compassion, wisdom, and guidance of Spirit. It's an invitation. You're letting go of control, and you're inviting Spirit in to help you be the loving adult that you need to be to move into step 3.

Let's say that you have a child who is crying and upset. If you say to the child in a harsh, judgmental voice, "What's wrong now?" is the child going to feel safe enough to let you in? No. That's why it's so important to be a loving adult. We can't be going in and saying to ourselves in the judgmental voice of the wounded self, "What did I do now? What's going on now?" It's like with a child. A child will feel safe when we say in a calm and nurturing voice, "Honey, I know you're upset. There must be a very good reason that you're upset. Is there something that I've done that upset you?" It's an openness. It's creating a safe space. That's what we need to do on the inner level: create a safe space for our inner child to be open with us. If there's any judgment, there's not going to be openness.

Sometimes we can just decide to open when we feel anxious or depressed. It's easy, and we just go right through the steps. Sometimes we get stuck; we can't really get to that openness.

There are some things that you may need to do to open yourself when you're in a stuck place. I call them *bridges to openness*. You may need to take a walk. You may need to be in nature. You may need to go to a Twelve-Step meeting. You may need to call a friend, play with a pet or a child, watch something funny, meditate, or pray. Sometimes even those things won't do it because we get stuck in anger and blame. We say, "This isn't my issue. I'm feeling upset because so-and-so did such and such. I'm not the one who's causing my pain. It's that this person yelled at me or this person judged me. It's really not me." It's easy to go into the place where you're not taking responsibility. That's not an openness to learning.

We have a powerful, three-step process for moving through getting stuck behind anger, called the Inner Bonding Anger Process. Not everybody will need to bring it into their lives, because not everybody gets stuck behind anger. Some people just don't feel angry. If you don't find this process helpful to you, that's fine. I've used it a lot in my life. I used to get angry often, and I found this process to be extremely helpful.

People have been dumping out anger in different anger processes for years: hit with the bat and get mad at your parents, or get mad at whoever. Research shows that nothing changes; in fact it even gets worse. Just dumping out anger doesn't get you anywhere.

This three-step process is different. We start out getting angry at somebody in the present. It doesn't even have to be anything major: maybe somebody cut you off in the freeway. It could be a partner, a child, or a parent. The second part is, you ask yourself, "Whom does this remind me of from the past?" You let your angry part go into the past and go at that person. You don't do it with the person there: you're doing it on your own. You can roll up a towel and beat the bed if nobody's around, or go in your car and yell it out. You can even whisper it out if you're not comfortable. You can write it out.

The third part is the most important. Here you let your inner child get angry at you for any way you're treating yourself in this situation—any way you're not taking care of yourself or treating yourself the way the people you're angry at might be treating you. We bring it back home. That's the big difference from just dumping out anger, because current anger at another person is a projection of some way that our inner child is angry at us for how we're not taking care of ourselves—how we are abandoning ourselves.

The wounded self loves to project. Projection means that you're putting what's really going on in you onto somebody else. If you're angry, you might think somebody else is angry, or it's their fault. If you're judging yourself, you might think somebody else is judging you. It's very common for the wounded self to project how we're treating ourselves onto other people. It happens often with anger.

Many people grew up in homes where there was anger or violence, so this process may be scary for you. It's important to understand that there are two kinds of anger. One is anger that's meant to control. This is dangerous anger. It can go into violence and other horrible things. The second kind is anger with an intention to learn. It's not meant to hurt or control anybody; it's about learning. You want to reassure your inner child that this anger is not dangerous anger. That will help you to hang in for the process.

I was raised in an angry, household, and I learned to be like a deer in the headlights. I would freeze when my mother got angry at me. I wouldn't know what to do. It's still hard for me when people get angry at me, but now I've learned to deal with it. I don't freeze. I don't give myself up. I show up as a loving adult. I can still feel the anxiety, because it never feels good when somebody's dumping their anger on you, but now I know how to manage it.

Reassure your inner child that this is not going to be a dangerous situation for you. This is a learning situation. This is not closed, controlling anger. This is anger that's open to learning.

Our assistant will demonstrate the anger process, and I will help her through it.

Assistant: I'm angry with my daughter because it's been two and a half years since we've spoken. She's not letting me see my grandchildren. I feel a huge loss. We saw each other the other day at a restaurant, and we talked on the phone a little bit, but it's been two months since she's contacted me, and I've reached out to her. I feel really angry that it's not important to her to heal our relationship and work through the problems she has. We haven't been getting along, and I feel angry with her about that.

Margaret: OK, so go for it. With the anger process, there's no holds barred, other than you can't hurt anybody and you can't hurt yourself. You can curse. You can scream. You can yell. You can kick. You can do anything, but you can't hurt yourself or anybody else.

Assistant: (yelling) I feel really angry at you, because you're being such a bitch. You won't let me see my grandkids, and I love them. You won't act like a loving person. I miss you, and I want to see my grandkids, and I don't understand why you're treating me like this, because I've always been a good mom to you. Now you're treating me like I don't matter, and it really hurts me. I'm so upset; I don't know what to do. I don't know how to fix it. I want to fix it, but you won't let me fix it. You won't let me be part of your life, and you're being a bitch to me.

Margaret: OK, good. Now, who in the past does this bring up?

Assistant: I'm feeling my dad come up.

Margaret: OK, go ahead.

Assistant: (yelling) Dad, you weren't around. You left when I was little. Where are you? Where have you been? I don't understand why you left me. You don't love me, and I don't know why you don't love me. Why don't you love me? I just want you to be here. I want you to love me and take care of me, and you just left us with our mother and never looked back. You don't care what the hell happened to us. You only care about yourself. You're just selfish, selfish, selfish. All you ever cared about is yourself, and you never paid attention to us. You weren't around for us. You left just like we didn't even exist. Nobody existed. I don't exist to you.

Margaret: OK, good. Now let your little girl get angry at you when you are being your wounded self.

Assistant: (yelling) You never hear me. You don't hear what I have to say. All I want you to do is to hear what I have to say. You can't hear me. You don't love me. I just want you to love me and care about me and be there for me and stand up for me and help me figure things out and solve all the problems. You're just never there for me. All you do is leave me all alone.

Margaret: Good, so breathe that in.

This process brings the anger home so that it's not about her daughter. It's not about her father. It's about how we treat ourselves. Of course, even though our wonderful assistant has been on this path for a while, it *is* a path. Sometimes she takes care of herself; sometimes she doesn't. When she doesn't, her little girl's mad at her. Right?

Assistant: Yes.

Margaret: That's the way it is. Thank you.

Assistant: You're welcome.

Margaret: Now, I hope you go through the process for yourself. Start with someone in the present, then go into the past, to somebody in your past whom this reminds you of. Let your inner child get angry at how you treat yourself.

The Inner Bonding Anger Process

1. Get angry at someone in the present.

2. Get angry at someone in the past that reminds you of the present person or situation.

3. Finally, come back into the present and let your inner child do the same things with you, expressing your inner child's anger, pain and resentment toward you for your part in the situation, or for treating yourself the way the people in parts 1 and 2 treated you. This brings the issue home to personal responsibility, opening the door to exploring your own behavior.

It's important to remember that this anger process is actually part of step 2 of Inner Bonding. It's part of getting yourself open. It's a really good thing to do if you're doing an Inner Bonding process and you're stuck and can't get yourself open.

Questioner: What do you do when a lot of infuriating situations have come up, and you haven't been allowed to voice your anger? Over the years it's been buried and has turned into depression and anxiety. You're quiet, and you hold it all in. I don't even know where to find it. Honestly, I have nowhere to find it.

Margaret: To find what?

Questioner: The anger.

Margaret: You don't need to find it. You need to focus on the anxiety and the depression and see how that's being caused by how you're treating yourself now.

We don't have to go looking for anger. If you feel angry, then you do the anger process, but not everybody uses anger as a cover-up for other feelings. If you're aware of anxiety, then you do Inner Bonding with the anxiety. If you're aware of depression, you do Inner Bonding with the depression. The anger process is for when you can't open to learning because anger is blocking you. As I said, not everybody is blocked by anger. You don't have to go looking for it.

To do the anger process when you're at home, you can roll up a towel and hit the bed. You can go in your car or into the closet, or somewhere where you won't be heard.

The three-step anger process can be very helpful for moving through whatever is stopping you from being open to learning. But it's not an end in itself. When you've gone through it, go into step 3.

Ivanka: I am very well aware of my anger and where it came from and how in the present it reminds me of the past and takes me there. I'm very well aware of how I feel when I get there. I snap, and I yell and scream, at times destructively. I throw things or break things. I'm very well aware that in that situation, it's panic mode. I don't like how my heart rate ramps up or how I feel. I can't speak. I stutter. It's a horrible time to be in. After the fact, I realize that I don't want to express my anger this way, but I don't understand how to stop it.

Margaret: What do you think is causing you to behave like that?

Ivanka: I think I don't know any better. My dad used to yell a lot, and my brother used to yell a lot. They would be superdestructive, so I grew up around it. My brain is programmed to express it like that.

Margaret: OK, but that's not why you're getting angry. Step 3 is *why* you're getting angry. There's some way that you're not taking care of yourself. Your little girl is angry at you and then projecting it out onto other people. Yes, you learned it in your family and all that. I learned it in my family too, but I don't get angry anymore.

Ivanka: How do you stop it?

Margaret: I don't have to stop it. It's not where I go. I go inward to take care of my little girl, not outward. Anger at other people is a form of control. You're trying to control them. You're dumping your feelings on them. You're making them responsible for you. As you develop your adult, and you really take care of yourself and your own feelings, you don't need to project it out onto other people.

That's what step 3 is about. It's about how you are treating yourself that's making your little girl angry at you, then projecting it out onto other people and blaming them for what's going on inside of you.

Ivanka: So you think that arguably I am snapping or getting angry at other people because my inner child is angry at myself.

Margaret: That's right, but you're not going inside and letting your inner child get angry at you. When you're snapping at somebody else, in some way you're abandoning yourself. Do you want to work on that?

Ivanka: Yes.

Margaret: What's a situation where you would get angry?

Ivanka: I work in a very stressful work environment. Two days ago, I was sick, my toddler was sick, and my husband was sick. We all got sick at the same time. I came from work pretty worked up, pretty stressed out.

We had a toddler who was not sleeping and wanted to nurse. I was extremely tried; I am thirty-four weeks pregnant. He was up, was crying, and I was trying to put him back to sleep. At some point, I said, "I can't nurse you anymore. I'm tired. It's 2:00 a.m. You're not sleeping. I'm tired."

He didn't take it. He was crying and crying, and I was holding him and talking to him. He is a toddler, twenty-two months old, so he probably didn't understand anything. I'm saying, "I'm tired. I really want to sleep," but he was crying and crying.

Finally, my husband, who was sleeping in a different room, walked in, and snapped in the middle of the night. He said, "Oh, my gosh, what are you doing? You're not doing anything. You're just sitting there and letting him cry and cry. Do something about it." Then my mom walked into the room, and she started yelling at me too: "You people. What are you doing? He's crying. You're not doing anything."

At that moment, I snapped. I yelled at him. I asked him to leave the room. I said, "You're not helping me in any way right now." I hated that moment because of how it made me feel. That was the one thing I didn't want my son to have, because I grew up with it. I know how it makes me feel.

Margaret: OK, so let's back up a little bit. You come home from work. You're not feeling well. Your mother lives with you.

Ivanka: She's helping me right now.

Margaret: OK, but was she sick?

Ivanka: No.

Margaret: But your husband was sick?

Ivanka: Yes.

Margaret: And your toddler was sick?

Ivanka: Yes.

Margaret: And you were sick.

Ivanka: Yes.

Margaret: OK. If you had been taking care of yourself, before all this happened, what could you have done differently to take better care of yourself, given that your mother was there and she wasn't sick?

Ivanka: I probably would have slept for more than four hours.

Margaret: You could have asked her to take care of him?

Ivanka: Yes.

Margaret: OK, so do you see that you didn't take care of yourself?

Ivanka: True.

Margaret: That's where the anger comes from—from not having taken care of yourself. If you had come home and said to your guidance, "I'm not feeling well. I'm pregnant. My son still wants to nurse. What would be loving to me?"

Ivanka: I would expect my husband or my mother to see that.

Margaret: Yes, but that's the problem. You've got an expectation that they're going to come and take care of something instead of speaking up, going to your mother, and saying, "I'm worn out. I'm sick. I need you to take over."

Ivanka: Sure. I would have reacted to it differently if I'd been feeling better.

Margaret: But you were sick and pregnant. It's a very hard situation, but you didn't take care of yourself.

Ivanka: True.

Margaret: That's where the anger comes from. That's what I'm trying to say: we get angry when we don't take care of ourselves. You could have said to your husband, "Look. I can't take any more. You're going to need to take over." You could have said it to your mother. Either of them could have taken over, but you gave yourself up. It wasn't working with your son. When they came in, asking, "What are you doing?" you took it out on them. Right?

Ivanka: Yes. It's very hard not to, though. Even in situations where I think I have control and I think I'm calm and quiet, if something is going at me, like my husband just going on and on . . .

Margaret: OK, but then you're not taking care of yourself. See if you can go inside and ask, "What is it about asking for the help I need instead of expecting somebody to notice?"

Ivanka: Because there was no one to help me.

Margaret: That might have been true when you were a child, but today, what are you telling yourself that leads you to not ask for the help you need?

Ivanka: It won't get done if I don't do it.

Margaret: Are you saying that if you asked your mother to help, she wouldn't?

Ivanka: She probably would.

Margaret: OK, so there's a false belief, isn't there? You're coming from a false belief: "I have to do it. I have to do it all. Nobody's taking care of me. Nobody's caring about me. Nobody's noticing." That's all coming from your wounded self. That's why you end up—

Ivanka: Snapping.

Margaret: Yes. You want to be noticing. That's what step 3 is about. It's about "How did I not take care of myself?" Does that make sense to you?

Ivanka: Yes. Definitely.

Questioner: You're saying that when you're angry at somebody, in reality you're just angry at yourself.

Margaret: Your inner child is angry at you for not being a loving adult with yourself and not taking care of you.

Questioner: So how do you make sure not to go that way versus saying, "It's my fault"?

Margaret: That's what the wounded self does. The wounded self will either blame somebody else or blame yourself. There's no learning in that. That's not an intention to learn. Blaming yourself just gets you off the hook. You can blame yourself, but you're not taking responsibility for learning about how you're abandoning yourself. Blaming yourself by telling yourself it's your fault is just another form of self-abandonment. If your intention is to be loving to yourself, then you're going to look at how you're abandoning yourself without any self-judgment. Blaming yourself can lead to projecting anger out onto others.

Questioner: What if the anger is only directed at yourself? I don't get angry at other people, but I am always angry at myself. I'm very full of negative self-talk.

Margaret: That's the same thing. That's the wounded self trying to control by judging you. In fact, it's one of the main ways the wounded self tries to control you. As we get into steps 3 and 4, you can explore that. What is your belief about being hard on yourself, judging yourself, being angry at yourself, blaming yourself? What do you hope to gain by doing that? You learned that form of control a long time ago, and there's a belief attached to it. It would be a very good thing for you to explore.

Step 3: Understanding the Inner Child and the False Beliefs

In dialoguing in step 3, the loving adult is coming from compassion, from curiosity. The loving adult wants to understand what we're doing that's causing any wounded feelings, as well as what's happening with another person or situation that may be bringing up core feelings.

As I've said previously, you don't want to do Inner Bonding in your head unless you're with somebody, and you're just trying to deal with it in the moment. Otherwise, you want to do the process in writing or out loud, because it'll keep you on track.

When you're dialoguing in step 3, let's say you come upon a false belief. You want to go right to Spirit and ask, "What's the truth?" Then you can come back to exploring if you want. If another belief comes up, again, you can ask, "What's the truth?" You're going back and forth between steps 3 (inner dialogue) and 4 (dialogue with your divine guidance), because you don't want to wait to discover the truth about a false belief.

It's very important to pay attention to both wounded feelings and to the existential core feelings of life. Let's take a feeling like fear. Fear can come from the wounded self when you are scaring yourself by saying things like, "This or that bad thing is going to happen." The wounded self loves to focus on the past and the future: any time you're in the past or future, you know you're in the wounded self. It loves to predict the future, as if it knows what's going to happen, and it'll say things that scare you: "You're going to mess up"; "you're going to lose your job." That fear creates anxiety and stress in the body (which is obviously very bad for the immune system).

Then there's also the existential core fear, which is a fear of real and present danger—something dangerous occurring right now. Let's say you're walking down the street, and suddenly the hairs on your neck stand out, and you get a sense of dread. You want to pay attention to that, because your inner guidance could be letting you know that there's a real and present danger.

There's a little story about a man who is walking through a forest at twilight, and he can't clearly see what is ahead of him. All of a sudden, he gets a feeling of dread, but he doesn't pay any attention. He walks a little further and again gets the feeling of dread, but doesn't pay attention. He walks a little further and falls off a cliff. He should have paid attention, right?

You want to pay attention to core feelings, because they can tell you some very important things about a person or a situation. In his book *Blink*, Malcolm Gladwell discusses how you can get much information in an instant—in a blink of an eye—if you're paying attention to your intuition. He tells the story of the Getty Museum, where somebody brought in a statue and said it was extremely ancient. Scientists tested it for a year and a half and decided that it was authentic, so the museum paid millions for it. Then they brought in a few art dealers, who were very sensitive, and within seconds, they knew it was a fake. The scientists went back to it and realized that the man who sold it had discovered a way of creating a patina on an object that was only a few months old. The scientists couldn't get what the art dealers knew in a second because they could feel it. One of them said, "It just feels too fresh." You want to learn to pay attention to this sense: there's so much information in it.

In step 3, the loving adult is asking questions, such as, "What am I telling you, or how am I treating you, that is causing your anxiety (or depression, guilt, shame, anger, aloneness, emptiness, jealousy)? What am I doing or not doing? How am I abandoning you?" Then you focus inward, allowing your feelings—your inner child—to answer.

Once you understand what you are doing to cause your wounded feelings, then you go deeper, into the wounded self: what are the beliefs, where did you get these beliefs, and why do you continue to believe them? You're asking the wounded self, "What are you trying to control or avoid or protect against by acting from this belief?" Because that's what the wounded self is doing, and that's what you want to discover. This is where the false beliefs are.

You don't have to worry too much about following rules: this is a fluid process. People worry about whether they're doing it right. Don't worry about that. Just be aware of your intention. If you're open to learning, if you're really intent on loving yourself, you're going to discover important information.

The wounded self wants to do everything right. Yes, there are Six Steps to help you along the path, but let them be more fluid. Don't be rigid about it. Once you ask a question, you want to go inside. If there's anxiety, you want to go into the anxiety: you want to focus inside your body, and let the answers come from the feeling itself, not from your head. Too often you ask a question, go in, and think, "Now I've got to figure out the answer." No: you don't want to be figuring anything out; you want to let the answer come from the feelings themselves. This is not a figuring out process. The wounded self always wants to figure it out, but you can't. It has to come from inside, from the feelings.

As I said, the loving adult is basically asking, "What am I when I'm acting as the wounded self, I telling you? How am I treating you? What am I doing or not doing that's causing you to feel this way?"

As you go deeper, you ask the wounded self, "What are the good reasons you have for thinking and behaving like this? Where did you get this belief? Where does this thought come from? Where does this judgment come from? What are you trying to control or avoid? What are you trying to avoid feeling?"

You're going through layers of trying to understand what you're doing and why you're doing it. How are you treating yourself, and why are you treating yourself this way?

Step 4: The Truth about Your Beliefs and the Loving Action

Once you get a clear picture of this inner situation, you go to step 4 and ask, "What is the truth about any of these beliefs, and what is the loving action toward myself?"

Sometimes it's helpful to do a very simple action, like picking up your inner child—a doll or stuffed animal or pillow—and hold that child. Bring some compassion in. That might be the first step you have to take: just to be present with yourself with compassion. As you get further into the process, loving actions can take many different forms, such as going back to school, changing jobs, or moving. It may be changing your diet, stopping an addiction, or speaking your truth with someone. Loving actions can be all kinds of things, but it's never going to be something that you don't really want. It might not be easy, but it will be loving to you.

People are often afraid that if they open to their guidance, they're going to be told to sell everything and go on some kind of a mission when that's not what they want to do: "If I open to guidance, it's going to try and control me, and tell me to do things I don't want to do, like leaving my relationship or my job."

It doesn't work that way at all. You're never going to be told to do something that you don't really want to do, because our higher will is the same as our inner will. In other words, there's not some being out there with an agenda for us. We're going to be guided to what we really want. What would really bring us joy? What's really in our highest good?

That doesn't mean it won't be hard. Sometimes it is hard, but it's still what you really want. It's important to understand that guidance is not somebody out there, deciding for you what you're supposed to be doing with your life. It's not like that at all. Our true will is the same as our higher will. We're just tapping into it, because we might have been ignoring our own real will—what we really want.

Step 5: Taking Loving Action

Step 5 is taking loving actions: whatever you've been guided to do by your higher guidance. Without taking loving action, none of the other steps mean anything. Sometimes you can take the action immediately, like holding your inner child or practicing staying present in your body. At other times, it might be an action that you take in a particular situation, such as saying no in a situation where you have been giving yourself up.

Step 6: Evaluating Your Actions

In step 6, you want to go back in, like in step 1, and see how you're feeling. If you're feeling some relief, if you're feeling less ashamed, less guilt, less anxiety or depression, you know you've taken a loving action.

Sometimes loving actions end up feeling worse in the short term. For example, if you want to stop drinking, smoking, or eating sugar, it's going to be hard; you're not going to feel great at the beginning. You have to go through a kind of detox, and it feels bad.

With some loving actions, you have to look at the long-term good feeling, not the short-term good feeling. At first, you're not going to feel much relief if you stop smoking. But in the long term, you know that it's going to be a whole lot better for your body. So we want to not only evaluate the short-term good feeling—are we feeling relief from a specific loving action?—but also the long term feelings.

When you're doing an exploration, you can start in a number of places, for example, with what are you feeling right now, or an issue or problem at work or with a child or a friend. You can also start with a past situation you want to understand more. You can start anywhere you want.

At this point in my life, I've dealt with so many issues that I just start with where I am presently. In the morning, I tune into my inner child and ask, "How are you doing?" If she says, "Fine," then I go right to my guidance. But sometimes she says, "I'm feeling uneasy." Then I'm going to go in and explore that. What's that about?

At this point, think about where you want to start with your exploration. Do you just want to start with what you're feeling right now? With a feeling that you often have, but maybe don't have right now? With a situation that you're dealing with?

Sometimes it's helpful to imagine that the part of you that's asking is your higher guidance. You can say to your guidance, "You be the loving adult and ask through me." In fact, this is very helpful if you procrastinate and don't do what you feel you want to do: ask your guidance to do it through you. You'll be amazed at what can happen if you get yourself out of the way and ask your guidance to act through you. The guidance can't act on its own, because it doesn't have a body, but *you* have a body, and you can invite guidance in to act through you.

Like anything worth learning, this process takes practice, so don't expect yourself to be good at it immediately. Please don't be hard on yourself or place a lot of expectations on yourself. I just want to encourage you to keep practicing.

If you're like most people, who are very busy, you may not want to devote extra time to this process. You don't have to. You can practice in the shower, while you're waiting in line at the market, or stuck in traffic. There are so many times to practice Inner Bonding. I do my morning Inner Bonding when I'm taking a walk, or when I'm in the shower or waiting in line. It's just a quick check-in: "How are you doing, honey? Anything you want to tell me?" What's most important is to keep practicing step 1: staying present in your body throughout the day.

Inner Bonding doesn't have to be time-consuming, although at times it can be. When life brings up new issues that I haven't dealt with before, I need to spend some time finding out what's loving to me, so it takes a little more time. But Inner Bonding doesn't have to be a very time-consuming process, so don't let your wounded self say, "This is so hard, and I don't have time to do it."

8

Guided Inner Bonding

Let me take you through the steps of Inner Bonding. You can do the process step-by-step as you're reading, you can have someone read it to you, or you can record yourself reading it and play it back to yourself—whichever feels most comfortable to you. Be sure you have some paper and a pen.

Start with step 1. Take some deep breaths, breathing in, using your breath to take you down inside your body. Start with whatever you're feeling right now, or with feelings about a situation that's of concern to you. Find the place in your heart that wants responsibility for your feelings.

Step 2: Now breathe into your heart, con-sciously choosing the intention to learn. Let go of theory, of doing it right or wrong. Just get out of your head and into the experience.

Imagine your higher guidance and invite the love and compassion of your guidance into your heart. Feel yourself opening to being a loving adult—kind, compassionate, open to learning, caring, loving, knowing that you have very good reasons for whatever you're feeling or however you are behaving.

Step 3: Ask your inner child in writing (again, using your nondominant hand might help you access your inner child more easily), "What am I telling you? What am I doing or not doing? How am I treating you that's causing this feeling?" Focus inside and let your inner child answer in writing.

Next, ask the wounded self, "What are you trying to control or avoid or protect against by treating a child this way? What is your hope for judging yourself, for ignoring your feelings, for numbing with addictions, and/ or for making others responsible for you?" As you become aware of the beliefs regard-ing the self-abandonment, explore where you got these beliefs. "What happened that led to these beliefs? How old were you when you concluded or absorbed these beliefs?"

Once you have a full understanding of what you are doing that is causing your pain and why you are doing it, move on to Step 4.

Step 4: imagine your higher guidance. You will generally ask two questions. If you've uncovered any false beliefs in the previous step, ask your guidance, "What is the truth?" Let go and open to receiving your guidance in words, pictures, or feelings.

Then move on to asking, "What is the loving action toward my inner child?" or, "What's the first thing I need to do to help my inner child feel that he or she is important to me?"

Then just open: make it OK for nothing to come. Just stay open to anything that wants to pop into your mind. Spirit communicates by popping thoughts, images, or feelings into our mind, so don't discount anything that pops in. It's actually not as hard as you think. Spirit wants to communicate with you. Spirit wants to help you, wants to guide you.

If you receive any information about taking a loving action, either take the action, or, if you can't immediately take it, imagine taking it, and see how that would feel.

I'd like you to imagine your guidance again. I'd like you to ask your guidance to tell your inner child something wonderful about who he or she really is. Let your guidance bring some love to your inner child, mirroring some of the beautiful qualities of your inner child. Tell yourself something wonderful about yourself.

As you learn and practice Inner Bonding, it's important to discern the difference between the voice of the wounded self and the voice of your higher self. How can you tell the difference? First, the voice of the wounded self will make you feel bad. You're going to feel anxious, tense. You're going to have wounded feelings. The voice of your higher self is never going to cause those feelings. If, as a result of the communication, you're feeling fear, anxiety, depression, guilt, shame, anger loneliness, or emptiness—any of these wounded feelings—that's not your guidance. That's your wounded self. Your guidance is going to bring relief.

Furthermore, the voice of the wounded self comes *from* your mind, but the voice of guidance comes *through* your mind. Spirit communicates

Dialogue Questions

Dialogue for wounded feelings of anxiety, depression, guilt, shame, anger, hurt feelings, jealousy, and so on:

The loving adult asks the inner child:

- What are you feeling right now?

- What am I telling you, and/or how am I treating you that is causing these feelings?

- How am I abandoning you?

- Have I been ignoring you by staying in my mind, not attending to your feeling?

- Am I judging you?

- Am I scaring you with lies or false beliefs?

- Am I turning to addictions to numb out your feelings?

- Am I giving you away to others, making others responsible for you?

- Are you angry with me? It's OK to be angry with me. I'd like to hear your anger.

- It's OK to cry. I'm here for you.

The loving adult asks the wounded self:

- What are you trying to control or avoid by judging, staying in your mind, turning to addictions, focusing on false beliefs, and/or making others responsible for your feelings?

- What is your belief about your ability to handle pain (or about your lovability, your ability to control others, your feeling responsible for others,

others' responsibility for you, your right to make
yourself happy, your ability to make yourself
happy, and so on)?

- Where did you get this belief? What childhood
experiences created this belief?

- What do you gain by acting as if this belief were
true?

- What are you afraid of in letting go of this belief?
What are you afraid would happen if you stopped
acting as if this belief were true?

Other questions you can ask your inner child:

- How do you feel about _____?
(Name a person)

- How do you feel about the work we do?

- I'd like to understand why you feel scared of
  _____.

- I'd like to understand why you don't like
  _____.

- Tell me more about that.

Sometimes present situations—people and events—
can touch off past experiences and create feelings of
anxiety, anger, pain and fear. When you become aware
of feeling these feelings, you can ask:

- Is something happening now that reminds you of
something that happened when we were little?

- Does this person remind you of mom, dad, a
brother or sister, a grandparent?

- Does this situation remind you of a traumatic experience that we had when we were little?

- I really want to know about everything you remember from the past. Your memories are very important to me, and I want to help you heal old fears and pain.

- Do you need me to provide us with someone to help with this? Do you need to be held while you go through this pain?

At times during the dialogue the loving adult may need to affirm how he or she feels about the child:

- I'm here for you right now, and I'm learning to be present for you.

- I love you, and your happiness is the most important thing in the world to me.

- You are so smart. Thank you for all this wonderful wisdom.

- Your creativity amazes me.

- It's truly OK for you to feel this anger, even if it's at me. I won't stop loving you no matter how angry you feel.

- You can keep crying as long as you need to. You are not alone. I'm here for you.

- It's OK to make mistakes. You are lovable even if you make mistakes.

- You don't have to do it "right." I will continue to love you no matter what you say or do, even if you say or do nothing at all.

The dialogue process can also help you become aware of what you want in everyday situations. You can facilitate this by asking your inner child questions such as:

- What are your favorite foods?

- What would you like for dinner tonight?

- What do you feel like wearing today?

- What are your favorite colors?

- Who do you like to spend time with?

- What would you like to do this Sunday?

- What were your favorite activities when you were little?

- What kind of books do you like to read?

- What kind of music do you like?

- What kind of movies do you like?

- What kinds of vacations do you like

- What kind of exercise do you like?

- What kinds of creative things do you like to do? Art? Crafts? Music? Writing?

- What are some of the things you've always wanted to do but have never done? Learn to fly? Learn to sail? Learn karate?

Dialoguing with your inner guidance:

- What is the truth about the beliefs I have uncovered?

- What is the loving action toward my child?

- What do I need to think or do differently to take care of my inner child?
- What is the real issue here?
- What do I need to look at about myself?
- What is my responsibility in this situation?

Inner Bonding with Your Painful Core Feelings

1. Put your hands on your heart. Compassionately embrace your feelings of loneliness, heartache, heartbreak, grief, helplessness over others, sadness, sorrow, or fear of real and present danger. Be very gentle, tender, caring, and understanding for these painful feelings.

2. When you are ready to release the feelings, give them to Spirit and invite in peace and acceptance.

3. Open to learning what these feelings are telling you about what is happening with someone or with an event or situation.

4. Open to learning with your guidance regarding the loving action in this situation.

5. Take the loving action.

6. Evaluate how you are feeling as a result of the loving action.

with us in many ways. Your guidance may take the form of images, pictures, or feelings rather than a voice. Some people only get the communication through dreams. They'll ask a question before they go to sleep, then they wake up with the answer.

Spirit will find a way to communicate with you. It might not be immediate. For me now, it's pretty immediate, but when I first started, sometimes it would take hours or days or even weeks before I would be able to access the answer. It wasn't because the answer wasn't there, but because my frequency wasn't high enough to access it. Now it's pretty quick but that's taken a lot of practice.

I'd like to suggest another exercise, which is for dealing with core painful feelings.

Think of a situation that causes you to feel heartache, heartbreak, loneliness, sorrow, grief, helplessness, or other painful core feelings.

As you think of this painful situation, cross your hands over your heart. Hands on the heart stimulate oxytocin, which is the feel-good hormone. Make sure that you're present in your heart with your guidance.

Say to your inner child, "Sweetie, I know that it really hurts your heart when that person acts that way, or with this great loss (of a person, a job, financial security). I know that it causes you such heartbreak. I understand how painful this is. I want you to know I'm right here with you. You're not alone. I'm not going to leave you alone. I'm going to stay with you for as long as you feel this pain. It's OK to feel this way. And I'm right here. I love you, I love you so much. I'm going to stay right with you. And it's perfectly OK to cry. Feel the feeling as deeply as you need to. I'm not going to leave you; I'll be right here with you the whole time."

It's really important to name the feeling. Your inner child needs to know that you know what this feeling is, that it's loneliness, heartbreak, grief, helplessness, or sorrow. It's really important for the inner child to hear that you know what this feeling is. There might be a core feeling from the past that you never let yourself feel.

Stay with it, holding the child who's feeling that feeling, until you start to feel the feeling is ready to release, at least for this time. Imagine that feeling being released to Spirit. Say, "I release this feeling to Spirit, and I ask you to replace it with peace and acceptance." And I breathe in the peace and acceptance. Just breathe that in. It doesn't take very long once you name the feeling and the inner child feels you there.

It might take a few minutes or much longer for this feeling to release, and, for big losses, it will come back many times. You need to do this practice every time the feeling comes back. Certain situations in life are very difficult. You want to show up like this for them every time they come up, with compassion, caring, tenderness, gentleness. This is what heals.

Once you release the feeling, move into an intention to learn with your guidance: What am I supposed to be learning about the situation or person? What information do I need from this? Don't just stop with the release of the feelings: go into the intention to learn, because there's always going to be something to learn. What do I need to learn regarding the person or situation? If it's about someone who has been hurtful to you, there's information about the person you might need. There may be a loving action you need to take, so ask, "Is there a loving action I need to take regarding this person or situation?"

Questioner: When you asked what I was feeling, I was actually feeling something positive and grateful. Where do you go then about the wounded self? Do you just congratulate yourself on the good feeling?

Margaret: When I check in and I feel fine, I go right to my guidance and ask an open-ended question: "What would you like to tell me?" Over time, you're going to find that your guidance has a lot to tell you. In fact, when I first started doing this, there was so much my guidance had to tell me that I took my tape recorder with me. When you check in, and you feel wonderful, grateful, and happy, go right to your guidance.

Questioner: When you suggested that we tell our inner child something wonderful, I could only say that I'm loved because I'm a child of God. It was the best I could do.

Margaret: As you spend more time with your guidance, you are going to see more beautiful qualities. And it's really important that you spend the time with your guidance seeing your inner child.

Questioner: I came here this weekend knowing I'm high-maintenance. I need to take time with myself, but I never realized how much time until now. It's almost 24/7.

Margaret: Yes, in terms of staying present, it is.

Questioner: Everything brings up issues and feelings and moods, so I take a lot of time and commitment to do this work. I'm willing to do it.

Margaret: Good!

Questioner: My dog is old and fading. I pet him and tickle him, and he'll turn around and give me his backside. He's not interested.

Margaret: What are you telling yourself at that moment?

Questioner: He doesn't love me.

Margaret: That's what you want to tune into: your wounded self is taking your old dog's behavior personally. You want to tune into that, because it's what's making you feel abandoned. It's not your dog turning his butt to you that's making you feel abandoned. You're telling yourself that from your wounded self: "My dog doesn't love me anymore." That's the lie that your wounded self is making up that makes you feel abandoned.

Questioner: Yes, and do you know how many lies I've listened to before?

Margaret: Yeah, but that's what you want to become aware of. It doesn't matter that it's your dog. In any situation where you feel abandoned, you want to go in and say, "What am I telling myself from my wounded self?" Whatever it is, it's going to be a lie because the wounded self has no access to truth. It makes things up all the time or operates from old programs like a broken record.

Questioner: My dog is old and he is dying, and I'm going to lose him. It's a lot easier for me to say he doesn't love me anymore and be upset about that than to be upset about the grief that will take place.

Margaret: That's right. That's covering up the grief.

Questioner: If that's the case, I have been listening to a lot of these lies, so that means I'm carrying a lot of core issues.

Margaret: That's right, they get stuck. When we don't deal with the core pain, it gets stuck. But when we deal with it, it moves through pretty quickly. You don't want those feelings to get stuck, because that stress can cause illness.

Kevin: I hit an unexpected roadblock. When I was listening to my guidance, I got a lot of good information. Then towards the end, my guidance said, "If you will let me in, I will walk with you. You don't have to do this alone." Immediately I thought, "Oh no, no! That's not OK!" I got really uncomfortable, so I went for a walk.

When I came back, I realized it what it is: I don't trust my guidance. I think there's a belief that I can't trust people, and I have to do this alone. How do I get past that roadblock so I can utilize my guidance?

Margaret: First of all, you need to realize that the part of you that doesn't trust is your wounded self. The wounded self never will trust. That's just who the wounded self is.

As I've already said, when I started, I had no trust. I had to test my guidance out—over and over again. I just had to take the risk.

This was one of my big tests; I'll never forget this time. I was doing an intensive in Missouri, and it was in the summer. It was really hot. They were serving lemonade at a break, and I actually heard a voice (I don't often hear an actual voice) that said, "Don't drink the lemonade; it's contaminated."

I looked around to see if somebody was talking to me, but there was nobody there. So of course my wounded self said, "Oh, you're crazy. You're making this up." I drank the lemonade, along with four other people, and we all got quite sick. It *was* contaminated.

I did test out my guidance personally over and over again through the years. I don't do that anymore. Now I know that my guidance is there, what it sounds like, and that it has my highest good at heart.

That's what you're going to need to do. You're going to need to take the risk of sometimes listening to your guidance and see what happens and sometimes not listening and see what happens.

Kevin: Then it occurred to me that there's actually another underlying situation: the fact that I never in my life met my father. I started to ask myself what was going on. I think I replicate the feelings of loneliness from that situation, and I put it on to others. Maybe I could do this exercise with my father for a while every day, because I think I have been projecting that situation onto other things.

When Spirit came to me, I got the message about what I could say to my inner child. It was very easy for me to say those positive qualities, and it was very easy for me to believe them. But it doesn't mean that there's these other situations that can't come. They come a lot.

Margaret: What kind of situation would come up?

Kevin: I work as a performer and actor, so I get rejected a lot. It's not always personal, but sometimes it gets really personal.

Margaret: Is it personal from the outside? Are they saying something personal, or are you making it personal?

Questioner: I'm making it personal. Usually we work with male directors. They get mad; they tell me what to do and how to say things. I'm aware that this is what they've hired me to do, but I don't do it. As it's happening, I know that there is something else going on that has nothing to do with the person in front of me.

When I was driving here, I started having resentments about you—money grabbing, giving me marketing calls after getting my money. I knew I was doing it; obviously it had nothing to do with you; I don't even know you. I knew that that was my ego, my wounded self, talking, not wanting to get what I was going to get here. When I'm in those situations, sometimes it's very scary for me, because it inhibits the creative process.

Margaret: I'd like you to take some deep breaths. Scan your body right now; notice what you're feeling inside. What do you feel physically right now in your body?

Kevin: I feel a little tight right here.

Margaret: Breathe into that tightness. Get present within. Decide that you want responsibility for that feeling. Can you do that? OK, now breathe into your heart and open to learning about loving yourself, about how you're treating yourself. Invite in the love and compassion that is your guidance, so that for right now you're a loving adult. I want you to ask your little boy: how do you treat him? Like your father, whom you never met? Like your father, who disappeared? How you treat him makes him mad.

Kevin: I ignore him. I pretend he's not there.

Margaret: It's kind of like your father: you weren't there. Your wounded self is retraumatizing your little boy by acting as if he doesn't exist. Is that right? When the director is telling you what to do, it sounds as if your little boy is projecting onto the director how you're treating yourself and how your father treated you by disappearing. It obviously has nothing to do with the director, but your little boy has to express it somewhere. If you're completely ignoring him, it's going to come out—at me, at the director, somewhere.

Kevin: When you were talking about step 1, I was feeling very good, because I realized that I need just to be present with little Kevin. For the whole day, I've been feeling that if I can connect to that space, to him here, it's almost like I feel home.

Margaret: Yes, that's right.

Kevin: That seems a little too easy.

Margaret: People always say that like it's supposed to be really hard. Feeling whole lets you know that you're loving your little boy. The difference between being in your head, ignoring him, and being present in your body with him is night and day. It might seem simple, but it's not always easy.

Kevin: So I would like to ignore my inner child partly because those feelings are painful?

Margaret: Yes. The fact that you never knew your father causes a lot of pain, a lot of grief. Of course you didn't want those feelings, so you learned to ignore them rather than being with them. But now you can handle those feelings. When you do, it's the difference between never meeting your father and your father being here, picking you up, and holding you. That's a big difference, right? Now you're the father. You're the one who can do it.

Kevin: My wounded self is saying now, "Is she crazy?"

Margaret: Say to your wounded self, "Honey, you don't know what you're talking about. Just step back."

Kevin: Yeah, I've been able to start to do that, because it comes up strongly, but I respond, "You know, wounded self, thanks for your feedback, but—"

Margaret: Don't say thanks, because you don't want the feedback. No, just say, "You need to be quiet. You need to step back. You don't know what you're talking about."

Kevin: It's lies.

Margaret: Yeah, it lies, it always lies. It sounds like you know what the loving action is: just to get present, be present, with your little boy in a way that your father never was.

Or, probably, your mother. But now you can. That's wonderful, Kevin.

Questioner: I'm finding it very hard to surrender control in practical matters. I feel I cannot surrender control because it's going to affect so many practical things; do you know what I mean?

Margaret: What would be a practical matter?

Questioner: I'm very controlling over our daughters regarding what they eat.

Margaret: Who buys the food in your home?

Questioner: Me.

Margaret: Good. I bought the food in my home, and that gave me the right to control it. In my home, when I was raising my kids, nutrition was very important to me. Since I was the one that bought the food, I was the one that had the right to control it.

It's not that control is bad. There's nothing bad about control. But when you're trying to control things that you have no control over, that creates a problem. I had total control over what came into the house, but I had no control over whether my kids traded their lunches at school or used the money they earned to buy junk. I didn't even try to control that. It's a waste of energy to try to control something over which you actually have no control.

That's where we get into problems. We try to control how people feel about us, how they act, how they treat themselves. We have no control over that. But it's 100 percent fine for you to control what you bring into your house.

It creates all kinds of problems when you try to control things about kids that you can't. You can put good food in front of your children, but you can't make them eat it. In my house, I would only have good food. If I cooked a meal and put it in front of them, and they didn't eat it, OK, they didn't eat it. When they got hungry, they would get something else. But there was only good food in the house, so that's all they could get, and it was fine with me to have complete control over that.

Questioner: I'm currently heartbroken and not getting over a breakup. I said, "What am I telling myself? I'm not lovable. It's all my fault." I know these are all lies. Then I asked myself your question: "What am I trying to control or avoid by treating my child this way?"

Margaret: It sounds like you're trying to control your feeling of heartbreak. By telling yourself you're not lovable, you're making it your fault, and you're going to feel anxious, depressed, guilty, ashamed, or alone. Those wounded feelings cover up the deeper core pain. The wounded self comes in and says, "I don't want to feel heartbreak; it's not OK to feel heartbreak; that's too hard. So I'll tell you that you're not good enough, that it's your fault, and that you're not lovable. Then you'll feel guilty or ashamed or wrong, but you won't feel heartbroken, because I will have come in to judge you, and that's going to cover it up."

Questioner: I feel like I'm still totally feeling the heartbreak, though. Am I?

Margaret: If you are, then you are not showing up for it as a loving adult, because it's not moving through you. You might be mostly feeling the pain of your self-judgment.

Questioner: For sure, I'm feeling that.

Margaret: OK. Accept that your wounded self is lying to you. It's not because there's something wrong with you, or because you're not lovable. Can you tell me a little bit more about your situation?

Questioner: This is going to be bad.

Margaret: See what you're telling yourself already?

Questioner: Because it's real.

Margaret: Oh, no, honey. Get yourself off the hook right now. Make it OK to just let happen whatever is going to happen right now.

Questioner: Oh, my God. OK.

Margaret: Can you tell us a little bit about this heartbreak situation?

Questioner: I was with someone with whom I felt an immediate connection. Bad news: I should not have been with him.

Margaret: How long ago was this?

Questioner: Two years ago, and we broke up with almost a year ago. He's funny, charming, sweet, and affectionate—all the good things. He's also very calm. My dad was very explosive, so I go for very calm men, who are tortured deep inside. He said all the right things, like "I've never known anyone like you," which I do believe is true. I'm from Florida, and he's from Northern Ireland. Very poetic, very creative, with beautiful ways of speaking. He was completely dependable; he was always on the spot, calling when he said he would, from the get-go from the first day.

Margaret: Then what happened? Why did the two of you break up?

Questioner: Oh, we broke up for many reasons. We're not a good fit, and he's alcoholic. He grew up in the Troubles in Northern Ireland. He grew up with a lot of violence—in a war zone.

Margaret: Did he break up with you, or did you break up with him?

Questioner: Oh, he dumped me. He cheated on me, and I think he was cheating on me many times. It was long-distance. I'm a tour director, so

I would go and stay there, but we'd still have a couple months without seeing each other. But we still talked every night; we video-chatted for three to four hours at night.

Margaret: When you met him, how long did it take to get into the relationship?

Questioner: Forty-five minutes. We were kissing within forty-five minutes. Wild-eyed, totally unhealthy, lots of red flags.

Margaret: What were the red flags?

Questioner: Alcoholism. Going too fast. He lied to me about when he had broken up with his wife. He said it had only been over a year.

He said that he was very open to talking about everything. What sent me over the edge for him was when he we had a big conversation, he said he liked to discuss everything and that he was not going to lie about things. He did seem to open up to me. He really did tell me things he had never told anybody else, which I do believe was true. He's very closed off.

He was very kind. There was a little boy that almost knocked over our pints at a bar in Belfast. My father would have exploded with rage or gotten totally annoyed. But he immediately said, "It's OK, it's OK." He was just so compassionate and sweet that it hooked me in. It's everything

I wanted, except for the lying and cheating and alcoholism.

Margaret: How much research have you done on narcissism?

Questioner: I've done a lot of research on narcissism. Are you saying he was a narcissist?

Margaret: It sounds like it. Everybody is somewhat narcissistic in their wounded self; that's garden-variety narcissism. But you're talking about symptoms of narcissistic personality disorder.

Questioner: He was never mean, though; he only built me up.

Margaret: But he wasn't living with you. It was a long-distance relationship. There's so much of what you're talking about: the lying, the drinking, the cheating, the coming on strong at the beginning, saying, "I've never met anybody like you"—that's such a typical line of a narcissist.

You get hooked in, because he was giving you something that you were not giving yourself. You're still not giving it to yourself, because you're still putting yourself down, you're still judging yourself, you're still blaming yourself, which makes you a sitting duck for somebody else to come along and say, "Oh, I've never met anybody like you; you're the most wonderful person."

Questioner: What if he *has* never met anybody like me?

Margaret: If that were true, he wouldn't have been cheating.

Questioner: He's cheated on everyone he's ever been with.

Margaret: That's right, because he's likely a narcissist.

Questioner: I don't feel his cheating was a reflection on me either.

Margaret: It's not a reflection on you. I'm not saying that. I'm saying that he knew the right things to say. If you go on YouTube, you'll see that they know exactly the right things to say to hook somebody in. They know how to be kind, act empathic, say exactly what you want to hear, and be wonderfully charming and poetic. I can't tell you how often I've had the same conversation with people who have been dumped by narcissists.

Almost anybody can get pulled in by a narcissist: they're very good at what they do. I've even worked with therapists who have been trained to understand what narcissism is but have gotten pulled in by narcissists, because they are so good at what they do.

But the real issue now is that you're putting yourself down and telling yourself that you're not good enough, you're not lovable, it's your fault, right?

Questioner: I am, deep inside. On the surface, I don't believe that's true, but deep inside I do believe it's true.

Margaret: That's right. So you're abandoning yourself rather than moving into compassion for how painful it is. It's painful to be pulled in by a very charming and smart narcissist and then be dumped by him. It's one of the most painful things that we can go through.

Questioner: I feel narcissists, though, are terrible people, and I don't feel he's a terrible person.

Margaret: They're generally not terrible people. They're just wounded people. There are malignant narcissists. He doesn't sound like a malignant narcissist, but much of what you are saying indicates that he's a narcissist. You might want to do more research and see what you come up with.

Questioner: I thought narcissists had to be always trying to tear you down, dominate you, and make you feel bad about yourself.

Margaret: That's generally true, especially once you live together, but he didn't live with you. If you have lived together, that might have been part of it. That might have been what happened in his marriage. Because he didn't live with you,

you didn't get to that point. I hope you do more research on narcissism. You're suffering because you're not understanding what really happened here. You're not understanding the deep heartbreak of somebody acting like that, giving you what you always wanted and then leaving. Realize that you need to be giving that to yourself, which you're not doing.

Questioner: It doesn't feel the same at all to like myself.

Margaret: Actually, if you were to really do it, you would be shocked at how great it feels.

Questioner: So that's just through practice.

Margaret: Yeah, it's practice. When you are really connected inside, you're really connecting with Spirit, and you're bringing love inside, you feel like you're going to float off the planet.

Questioner: I cannot even imagine it. I really cannot. It shows how disconnected I must be.

Margaret: But it is true. I couldn't imagine it either until I experienced it. That's the lesson here for you: when you start to give yourself what he gave you, you're going to start to heal.

Questioner: Then there's the other question: what is it you're trying to control or avoid?

Margaret: What are you telling yourself that's causing the feeling?

Questioner: I'm unlovable, a big disappointment. That's what he thought I was, and that's why he left.

Margaret: That's right.

Questioner: OK. So, then the next step is, what am I trying to control or avoid by saying those things to myself?

Margaret: Perhaps you're trying to not feel your helplessness over him. But you're causing more pain by saying those things to yourself than you would if you just felt the heartbreak and the helplessness. You're feeling the pain of your self-abandonment.

Questioner: Not of his abandonment?

Margaret: No. You're feeling the pain of your self-abandonment with your self-judgments. That's causing you a lot of pain.

Questioner: Yeah, because I'm really angry at myself and feel stupid.

Margaret: Yeah, and that's causing a lot of pain. If you were to let go of all the judgments, experience the deeper heartbreak of feeling that you had something wonderful, but it's gone, and attend to it with compassion, your helplessness over him would move through you; it would heal. You'd get the lesson that you need to start to treat yourself with love instead of what you're doing right now, which is complete self-abandonment.

Questioner: Yeah. Putting my hand on my heart was powerful. I really felt something; I don't know what, but something—I wouldn't say relief, but I felt nurtured.

Margaret: Right, but when you tell yourself, "It's your fault; you weren't good enough; you're a disappointment," that's hurting you. Say you had an actual little girl, and her father or some wonderful man told her, "You're the most wonderful little girl in the world, and I've never felt like this about any little girl before," and then he suddenly disappeared. Then you said to her, "It's all your fault. You're not good enough. You're a disappointment. You're not lovable." That's what you're doing to your little girl.

Questioner: Yeah, I see that.

Margaret: That's what's causing most of the pain right now. And not allowing the heartbreak and helplessness to move through. Your challenge is to start to start to give your little girl what he was giving you and then see how you feel.

Questioner: Is it the same with rejection? You just basically need to go through it?

Margaret: I don't even use the word *rejection*, because if somebody leaves or doesn't like me, I don't take it personally. I don't think it has anything to do with me, so I don't feel rejected. If I feel rejected, it's because I'm taking their rejecting behavior personally and thinking it's about me; then I'm rejecting myself. If somebody is being unloving or leaves, I don't feel rejected. That's their stuff. As long as I'm not rejecting my little girl, I'm not going to feel rejected by what other people do. Do you understand what I'm saying?

Questioner: Yeah, but if they tell you, "We don't want you anymore—"

Margaret: That's right, and how often are you telling yourself, "I don't want you; I don't want responsibility for you; I'm not going to take care of you"? How often are you rejecting yourself? If somebody says, "I don't want you anymore," to me that's just information about them. It has nothing to do with me. It's not about me.

Questioner: But it still causes cold feelings, right?

Margaret: I may feel sad. If that person was really important to me, I'd feel some heartbreak and helplessness over them. I would deal with that, but I wouldn't feel rejected; that's a different feeling. I don't feel rejected unless I'm rejecting myself. If somebody I really care about says, "I don't want to be with you anymore," I'm going to feel the hurt in my heart, because unloving behavior always hurts our heart, and I will show up with compassion for that. But I'm certainly not going to tell my little girl that it's her fault or that there's anything wrong with her. That's the rejection; that's the self-abandonment. That's you trying to believe that you have control over the other person, that if only you were good enough, then you could control how they feel about you. That's a major false belief of the wounded self.

Questioner: I thought that was taking responsibility for yourself.

Margaret: How is that taking responsibility?

Questioner: Like if I did better, or—

Margaret: That's saying, "If I did better, I could control how they feel about me. Oh, if only I were different, I could control that person," but that's not true. Self-responsibility is taking care of yourself regardless of what that person is doing. They're going to do what they're going to do. You don't control that. If somebody loves you for who you are and your essence, they're going to love you even if you mess up.

Questioner: There is a situation now that I'm feeling really sad about, and some of it is my fault, I know.

Margaret: Some of it might be your responsibility, yes, but it doesn't mean that you're a bad person. It wasn't your inner child who may have made a mistake, it was your wounded self, so judging your inner child and telling her she's not good enough is a lie. You're putting your wounded self in charge of the situation instead of your loving adult.

Questioner: So how do I get past it or through it now?

Margaret: You learn from it. You look at why you made the choices you did. What are the good reasons that you had for putting your wounded self in charge? You accept that there are consequences when you do that. You look at what you would have done if you had shown up as a loving adult, and you start to practice that.

Sometimes bad things have to happen, consequences have to happen, in order for us to finally say, "I'm going to show up as a loving adult; it's time to do that."

Questioner: What does the feeling of not being worthy have to do with it?

Margaret: That's your wounded self. That's the core of the wounded self: "I'm not worthy." The wounded self has no idea about your essence. None whatsoever. The wounded self isn't worthy, but the wounded self isn't who you are.

This is a very important point: We are not our wounded self. We are not our ego self. We created that as part of our strategy for survival, but we are not that. We are our essence, and the wounded self knows nothing about that. Your wounded self is telling yourself you're not worthy. That's what the wounded self will always do, and as long as you indulge your wounded self in that, you're going to feel unworthy.

When you put your loving adult in charge, you would never say that to your child. A loving adult would never say to a child, "You're not worthy; you're not lovable; everything is your fault." A loving, caring adult would never say that to a child in a million years. But you're indulging your wounded self in saying that, and that's hurting you. Do you see that?

Questioner: Yeah, I do. I know I have emotions. I guess I was confused about whether it's a core feeling or it's self-indulging.

Margaret: What are the emotions?

Questioner: Heartbreak.

Margaret: That's a core feeling, and you need to attend to it with a lot of compassion. But that's different than rejection.

Questioner: I have a commitment issue.

Margaret: So there's a place in you that's afraid to commit. Is that right?

Questioner: Yes.

Margaret: OK. I want you to breathe into that place. Where do you feel that resistance to committing in your body? Breathe into that and get present with it. What does that feel like inside?

Questioner: I'm constricting.

Margaret: So it's a tight feeling inside, that fear of commitment, choking tightness. Just breathe into that, be present with it. Are you willing to take responsibility? OK. Now breathe into your heart, open to learning, and invite your guidance in. Ask the part of you that's afraid of commitment, "You must have a very good reason for being afraid. Can you tell me what I do or don't do that scares you about commitment?" Then go inside.

Questioner: It just doesn't work out.

Margaret: OK, but what happens? When you go into a relationship, what do you do that ends up making your little girl fearful of commitment?

Questioner: Sabotage.

Margaret: How?

Questioner: Pushing it away.

Margaret: But you're pushing away for some good reason. What are you afraid of?

Questioner: Being abandoned.

Margaret: So you're going into a relationship with a fear of being abandoned by the other person, and then you're pushing the other person away rather than risk being open and getting hurt?

Questioner: I'm actually doing really well, not going to that place, but commitment does come up, like right now: I'm really choosing love and not the fear. But it seems at times that there's some inner chatter around this issue.

Margaret: People have two major fears when going into relationships. One is the fear of losing themselves. The other is the fear of losing the other person. And they're related, because people lose themselves in order not to lose the other person. They sacrifice themselves in the hopes of having control over not losing the other person.

Going into relationships with these fears is going to create a fear of commitment. So you're saying that you're aware that your fear is of losing the other person?

Questioner: Yes, but I also identify strongly with losing myself.

Margaret: That's right. The fear of commitment is that you're going to lose yourself in order not to lose the other person. That's what your little girl is afraid of, so she's afraid of commitment: "I'm afraid of commitment because I'm afraid that you're going to give me up in order not to lose the other person. And I'm going to get lost in the relationship."

What needs to happen here is developing a loving adult who would rather lose somebody else than lose yourself. Who has good boundaries against losing yourself. Who's willing to lose somebody else without falling apart, without feeling abandoned because you're not abandoning yourself. The more you learn to be a loving adult and not abandon yourself, the less afraid you are of commitment, because you're not afraid of losing either yourself or the other person. Your fear goes away when you know you can lovingly manage the pain of losing someone else, so you won't lose yourself to avoid losing the other.

When you're going into a relationship and your little girl is really scared, you're going to make the other person responsible. You're going to give yourself up to try to keep them from leaving you. What happens when they leave you? You're abandoned, because you've already abandoned yourself. But if you go into a relationship without making somebody responsible for you, without giving yourself up in order to control somebody, then, if somebody leaves, you've still got you.

Questioner: Yeah, I am really working in that space right there and it's making me go super-slowly, supercautiously. I see this whole issue with commitment working out so many times in my life, about not being able to make a decision on some-thing like a move. Even a trip. My daughter and I were planning to do a trip, and I couldn't commit to doing it.

Margaret: Yeah, but that's a different issue.

Questioner: That's not commitment?

Margaret: No, that's decision making. Fear of commitment in a relationship is coming from the two fears of being abandoned and abandoning yourself. Decision has to do with the fear of mak-ing the wrong choice. You don't know what choice to make. The problem is, you're trying to make the choice out of your head.

Here's how to make decisions. Imagine the sit-uation where you're going to go on a trip. First, you go inside and ask your little girl, "What trip do you want to go on?"

Questioner: A lot of places.

Margaret: Pick one.

Questioner: Africa.

Margaret: The little girl wants to go to Africa. Now go to your guidance and ask, "Is it my highest good to go to Africa?"

Questioner: Well, my responsible part says I can't afford it.

Margaret: So it's not in your highest good because it's too much money, right? Go back inside and say,

"I'm sorry, but it's too much money to go to Africa. Where else would you like to go that's not so expensive?" What comes up?

Questioner: Well, we're going to Puerto Rico.

Margaret: So you've decided to go to Puerto Rico. Then go to your guidance and ask, "Is it in my highest good to go to Puerto Rico?"

Questioner: I did the math; it worked out.

Margaret: So you have your decision. I make decisions really fast. I don't do them from my head at all. I go inside: "What do you want?" I go to my guidance: "What's my highest good?" When the two agree, there's my decision. It happens really fast. You're trying to decide from your head. That's what's getting in the way, but that's different than commitment.

It's important to make a commitment to yourself, a commitment to love. On our planet, energy is not local: it affects everything, so each of us affects everything. And the more we do our inner work and move into love for ourselves and each other, the more we help what's going on our planet.

Don't think that you can't affect what's happening. Don't think that you can't have a major effect, because each of us has the power to affect energy. There is the Hundredth Monkey theory, which originated in the 1970s, when scientists studying a group of monkeys on an island off Japan observed a group learning to wash sweet potatoes. One day, when about a hundred of the monkeys learned to wash their potatoes, suddenly the researchers found that all the monkeys in the region knew how to do it.

This experiment has been done in many ways: for example, teaching a dog a trick that dogs have never learned before. It would take, say, six months. Then they would take another dog in another place in the planet and teach them the same trick. It would take three months. Then they would repeat the process with another dog in another place; it would take him two weeks, because there's a collective unconscious or consciousness.

This is the collective consciousness. We tap into it. The monkeys on the other islands were tapping into the consciousness and learning to wash their dirty potatoes. We affect this consciousness. The more we do our inner work, and the more we learn to love ourselves, take responsibility for our feelings, and share that love with others, the more of a positive effect we have on our planet. If nothing else motivates you, I hope that that does, because I think that we each have a responsibility here on the planet to do all that we can to raise the frequency of our planet. It has to start with ourselves.

Resources

These resources are available at innerbonding.com. You can also find information on Events, including Intensives and support groups; Inner Bonding Village; and Facilitators and Facilitator Training.

Books

Healing Your Aloneness, 1990

The first book written on Inner Bonding. Takes you on a deep inner journey of healing. Helps you understand who the Child is, who the loving Adult is, and how to dialogue. Lots of examples.

Inner Bonding, 1992

Inner Bonding becomes a five step process in this next book. This book presents role modeling regarding how to take loving care of yourself in your relationships with your mate, friends, parents, children, and co-workers.

The Healing Your Aloneness Workbook, 1993
Teaches the Six Steps of Inner Bonding through many different exercises.

Do I Have To Give Up Me To Be Loved By God?, 1999
This book helps you heal any problems you have in your relationship with your Higher Power. It goes more deeply into the Inner Bonding process and teaches you how to have a direct, personal relationship with Divine Guidance—a relationship that heals emptiness, relationship problems, addictions, and leads to personal empowerment.

Do I Have To Give Up Me To Be Loved By You?, 1983
Describes how the intent to learn, as opposed to the intent to protect, leads to loving conflict resolution in committed relationships, and how conflict becomes the arena for creating learning, growth and passion.

Do I Have To Give Up Me To Be Loved By My Kids?, 1985
Shows how to move beyond authoritarian and permissive parenting into loving parenting from an intent to learn.

Do I Have To Give Up Me To Be Loved By You? . . . The Workbook, 1987
Helps you to discover the ways you protect against the pain you fear that actually creates your present pain.

Diet For Divine Connection: Beyond Junk Foods and Junk Thought To At-Will, Divine Connection, 2018
Discover how to experience a consistent, at-will connection with your spiritual source of love and guidance

The Inner Bonding Workbook: Six Steps to Healing Yourself and Connecting with Your Divine Guidance, 2019
A complete experience in learning and deepening your application of Inner Bonding to individual and relationship issues

Audio Tapes

Beyond Fear and Addictions
In this two hour tape set, I present an overview of Inner Bonding, bring you through the Six Steps in a visualization—including contacting your spiritual Guidance—and then I demonstrate the process with a volunteer from the audience. Questions and answers follow the demo.

Anger and Inner Bonding

In this tape I give a one hour overview of Inner Bonding where the Six Steps are acted out along with the three-part anger process that is part of Step Two.

Opening to Learning Meditation Tape

This is the 20 minute clearing and prayer that I do at the beginning of each day at an intensive. Each intensive participant receives one of these at the end of the intensive.

Do I Have To Give Up Me To Be Loved By Kids?

In this two-hour, 20 minutes set of tapes, we present how to parent children with an intent to learn and role play many different conflict situations, followed by questions and answers.

From Conflict to Intimacy and Beyond

This three-hour tape is exceptionally helpful in teaching the difference between the intent to protect and the intent to learn in conflicts in relationships. Much role playing different conflict situations.

Video Tapes

The Inner Bonding Introductory Lecture
This is a two-hour overview of Inner Bonding, along with the LifePaths charts. Extremely helpful to reminding you of the process and to introducing others to Inner Bonding.

The Master Teacher Connection
In this one hour and 45 minute tape, Erika describes how she sees the spiritual Master Teachers and some of what she has learned from her Teacher. Erika is an excellent speaker and this is a fascinating tape.

Courses

SelfQuest®
SelfQuest is a self-guided journey that takes place at your own pace, in the privacy of your own space. There will be challenges on this journey, but it is a journey well worth the effort because its invaluable rewards will last a lifetime. SelfQuest is a comprehensive educational, personal empowerment and conflict resolution completely encrypted online program.

Love Yourself: A 30-Day At-Home Inner Bonding Course with Dr. Margaret Paul

The $199 course includes videos and visualizations created just for this course, and a daily article. The $299 course also includes a special forum just for participants, and a weekly group call to get your questions answered. The call will be recorded so if you can't attend at the time, you will receive a copy of it. For about 15–20 minutes a day, you will learn Inner Bonding.

Unlocking Your Inner Wisdom

This course includes daily videos created just for this course and a daily lesson with an action step. For about 15–20 minutes a day, you can learn to connect with your inner guidance and your higher spiritual guidance, or deepen your current connection, and learn the art of manifestation.

Wildly, Deeply, Joyously In Love

This course includes a one-hour overview intro video, thirty 10–15 minute videos created just for this course, and a daily lesson with an action step. For about 20 minutes a day, you can learn how to heal your current relationship or how to create the relationships of your dreams, and you can take as long as you want to go through it. It's powerful for a couple, and for an individual, as it applies to all relationships.

Attracting your Beloved: A 30-Day At-home Experience with Dr. Margaret Paul to Learn How to Attract the Love of your Life
This course includes videos and visualizations created just for this course and a daily lesson. The upgraded course includes a special forum just for participants, and a weekly group call to get your questions answered. The call will be recorded so if you can't attend at the time, you will receive a copy of it. For about 20 minutes a day, you can learn how to attract the love of your life.

Passionate Purpose, Vibrant Health! A 30-Day at home Experience with Dr. Margaret Paul
This course includes videos and visualizations created just for this course, a daily article, a special forum just for participants, and a weekly group call to get your questions answered. The call will be recorded so if you can't attend at the time, you will receive a copy of it. For about 20 minutes a day, you can learn how access the blueprint for your passionate purpose and achieve the health and well-being to manifest it.

Complete Self Love the Ultimate Collection
In this course you'll get a master-level instruction on Inner Bonding, what it is, how to do it, and interactive tools that will help you apply this process in your everyday life to develop self-love.

The Power to Heal Yourself
Free Webinar with Dr. Margaret Paul Includes a special package called *The Power to Heal Yourself*

The Intimate Relationship Toolbox
This 12-week home-study course, which includes videos, audios and article packets, teaches you the Steps of Inner Bonding, while also teaching you how to create a loving relationship.

Dr. Margaret's Permanent Weight Loss Course
This 12-week home-study course, which includes videos, audios and article packets, teaches you the Steps of Inner Bonding, while also teaching you how to permanently lose weight.

About the Author

DR. MARGARET PAUL is a bestselling author, popular MindBodyGreen writer and co-creator of the powerful Inner Bonding® self-healing process, and the related Self-Quest® self-healing online program. She has appeared on numerous radio and tele-  vision shows (including Oprah). Her book titles include *Do I Have to Give Up Me to Be Loved By You* (and subsequent titles *Do I Have to Give Up Me to Be Loved By God, and . . . By My Kids*), *Healing Your Aloneness and Inner Bonding*, and the recently published, *Diet For Divine Connection* and *The Inner Bonding Workbook*. Margaret holds a PhD in psychology, is a relationship expert, public speaker, consultant and artist. She has successfully worked with tens of thousands and taught classes and seminars for over 53 years. Go to http://www.innerbonding .com/welcome for a free Inner Bonding course and join Dr. Margaret for her "Love Yourself" Course at http://www.innerbonding.com/show-page/224/ love-yourself-a-30-day-inner-bonding-experience .html.

She is a member of the Transformational Leadership council started by Jack Canfield.

Margaret lives in Colorado on a thirty-five-acre ranch. She has three children and three grand-children. In her spare time, she loves to paint, cook delicious healthy food, read, make pottery, and joyously live her life as a Golden Girl with her best friend.

Printed in the USA
CPSIA information can be obtained
at www.ICGtesting.com
JSHW012024140824
68134JS00033B/2865